Diverse Students, Diverse Outcomes

Diverse Students, Diverse Outcomes

Portal Schools for Access to Diverse Teaching and Learning

Frank S. Kelly

ROWMAN & LITTLEFIELD
Lanham • Boulder • New York • London

Published by Rowman & Littlefield
An imprint of The Rowman & Littlefield Publishing Group, Inc.
4501 Forbes Boulevard, Suite 200, Lanham, Maryland 20706
www.rowman.com

86-90 Paul Street, London EC2A 4NE, United Kingdom

Copyright © 2022 by Frank Kelly

All rights reserved. No part of this book may be reproduced in any form or by any electronic or mechanical means, including information storage and retrieval systems, without written permission from the publisher, except by a reviewer who may quote passages in a review.

British Library Cataloguing in Publication Information Available

Library of Congress Cataloging-in-Publication Data

Names: Kelly, Frank S., 1941– author.
Title: Diverse students, diverse outcomes: portal schools for access to diverse teaching and learning / Frank S. Kelly.
Description: Lanham, Maryland: Rowman & Littlefield, 2022. | Includes bibliographical references and index. | Summary: "The intent of Diverse Students, Diverse Outcomes is not merely to reiterate how to tweak the same things teachers and students have been doing for years but to engage them in exploring what school could be like in the future. Schools must restructure their facilities and teachers must draw upon a range of resources to help diverse students succeed"—Provided by publisher.
Identifiers: LCCN 2021057516 (print) | LCCN 2021057517 (ebook) | ISBN 9781475864700 (cloth) | ISBN 9781475864717 (paperback) | ISBN 9781475864724 (epub)
Subjects: LCSH: Educational change—United States. | Educational equalization—United States. | Academic achievement—United States. | Community and school—United States.
Classification: LCC LA217.2 .K45 2022 (print) | LCC LA217.2 (ebook) | DDC 370.973—dc23/eng/20211223
LC record available at https://lccn.loc.gov/2021057516
LC ebook record available at https://lccn.loc.gov/2021057517

Contents

Foreword	vii
Acknowledgments	ix
Introduction	xi
Chapter 1: Our Evolving Cities and Schools: Teaching and Learning Must Change	1
Chapter 2: Schools for the Future: Instruction, Technology, Time, Spaces, Community, Funding	15
Chapter 3: Creating Portal Schools	57
Chapter 4: Learning from Other Building Types	63
Chapter 5: Slow Learners?: Great Ideas and Great Schools Ignored	85
Chapter 6: Epilogue	113
Index	115
About the Author	121

Foreword

The time period in U. S. history between 1801 and 1890 is commonly known as the Westward Expansion movement. European immigrants streaming into the country came with the dream of land ownership and the opportunity to be upwardly mobile in life instead of being relegated at birth to a social class. After the Louisiana Purchase of 1803, more opportunities for individual land ownership became available. The Homestead Act of 1862 offered American citizens 160 acres of public land in western territories to settle and improve. It was the century when the ideas of the American Dream and Manifest Destiny were born.

In this period of massive migration, settlements began for a variety of reasons. Many sprang up and died within a few years, while others thrived and grew into communities. For a settlement to become a community, it generally meant that it had become a place for families and that required the establishment of two critical institutions—churches and schools. As more and more people sought the opportunity to own land and be independent, thousands of communities and schools grew across the country. So, early in our history as a nation and woven into the foundations of our culture, we find schools as a central institution of civilization and a marker of community success.

Also, beginning in the nineteenth century and dominating the twentieth century came the era of industrialization and the growth and migration to cities. Those migrants brought with them their value of the American Dream and the importance of education in making the dream become reality. Schools again became the center of communities within these metropolitan areas. Throughout the societal changes of the twentieth century, it is worthwhile to note that when communities, either rural or urban, lost the ability to sustain a healthy school, the community soon died or devolved into decay. Schools are a critical and emotional part of American infrastructure and culture. We only need to look at our own history to understand that a strong education system is an inextricable part of our DNA. As a nation, we cannot survive without it.

As with other parts of our lives, our love for something can oftentimes prevent us from making critical evaluations and needed changes to the detriment of the object of affection. The United States seeks to educate 100 percent of our population to a high degree of literacy and numeracy. Not all countries make this choice. As result, we have all been to school, and most of us look back at school with fond memories. We all tend to see a successful school through the lens of our own experience; therefore, the education profession can become fiercely resistant to change, not only among professionals but also the public at large.

It is common to hear individuals talk about "the way it was when I was in school." No other profession does this. In fields like aviation and medicine, we have made phenomenal advancements in technology and practice, and we make heroes of those who take the first steps in those innovations. Yet, in education, we often do the opposite and sometimes demonize those who would dare to change one of our foundational institutions. The consequences of such action or inaction endanger the progress of a vibrant society and strong country.

In *Diverse Students, Diverse Outcomes: Portal Schools for Access to Diverse Teaching and Learning*, author Frank S. Kelly provides a unique and timely perspective for how to approach the need to provide state-of-the-art teaching practice combined with the social-emotional development and community identity needs of our students and society. He explores the idea and points to tangible examples of schools serving as access points to high-quality academic opportunities regardless of physical location, combined with facilities and identities for extracurricular activities and social integration. It is an idea that makes sense and solves a number of issues around equity and opportunity for all students.

Frank S. Kelly provides a clear framework and practical examples of how such reforms can become reality. The challenge to readers is to open their minds and be willing to consider schools in a different paradigm from tradition. Imagine what can happen. Our world changes whether we want it to or not, and it is our responsibility to prepare our children for those challenges. If we prepare our students for the world we have lived in as adults, we are guilty of malpractice. We must prepare them for the world to come and the uncertainty it brings with it. Bringing the world to our students through the school as a gateway is an idea that makes sense, is practical, and is greatly needed.

Dr. James McSwain
Houston ISD Area Superintendent West

Acknowledgments

Contributors to the thinking and discussions that shaped this book:

- James McSwain: Houston ISD area superintendent and former Lamar High School principal
- Dr. Ian Jukes: InfoSavvy Group, author, keynote speaker, and international consultant
- Teresa Dossman and Debi Koch: educators at TEACH
- Carolyn Means: School Solutions consultant
- John Casbarian: interim dean, Rice School of Architecture
- Dr. Matthew Lenz: family physician, Medical Clinic of Houston
- Dr. Robert Furse: oncologist
- Patrick Gural: manager, Central Market Houston
- Pat Guseman: PASA demographer
- Larry Groppel: Moak Casey, school finances
- Bob Sanborn and Sara Moran: Children at Risk
- Vinson Lewis: principal, Kerr HS
- Pam Wells: Region IV

Introduction

Work began on this book several years ago with the intent of exploring ways to make schooling more appealing, interesting, and engaging, for both students and teachers, with the objective of realizing better outcomes for all concerned. Consideration was given to the nature of the students and cities our schools serve, and it was powerfully clear how remarkably diverse they are in terms of their ethnicities, languages, family incomes, and learning aspirations/interests, and how that diversity has changed in recent decades—and how it seems certain to change still more in the future.

Then, in 2020, the coronavirus pandemic struck and forced our K–12 schools and universities, in a matter of months, to fundamentally change how and where teaching and learning could occur. Amazingly, this huge challenge did not conflict with the schooling being envisioned, but gave the thinking great urgency. Concepts had already begun to characterize the ideal schools for the future as "portals," not places where specific teaching and learning must occur, but powerful gateways through which teachers and students work together to access, personally and digitally, the super diverse teaching methods, vast learning materials, and flexible time our evolving communities and students need. Recognizing the enormous investment schools have in existing teachers and facilities, the proposed "portal" concept preserves and enhances how these could more effectively realize teaching and learning without increasing the costs of our schools.

As ideas for the book developed, it was amazing to "discover" things that have been around us many years—but our schools had not recognized how aspects of them could really benefit education environments. Examples include an eleventh-century Gothic cathedral, a nineteenth-century French public market, a twenty-first-century U.S. supermarket, a school of architecture in a U.S. university, and how alike and different doctors and hospitals are relative to teachers and schools.

And, through the exploring/writing process, a list of twenty-eight existing high schools was compiled that are based on very creative ideas and have worked well for students and teachers, some for decades. This raised the question of how such successful creative schools could have had so little impact on the traditional schools that still serve the majority of our students.

But the really big goal here is that as you read this book, you will be stirred to think of other ideas for reinventing and improving education—and will see your own school and your own community from a different perspective.

Chapter 1

Our Evolving Cities and Schools
Teaching and Learning Must Change

This chapter explores the nature of today's cities and their populations and the related needs to change our approach to secondary school education. It briefly describes our enormous and continuously evolving urban cities—assemblies of multiple municipalities with multiple modes of transportation, diverse economies, and very diverse populations. It notes that they continue not only to grow, but to change where people live and work, and how these areas are typically served by multiple school districts, each with multiple schools, each with very diverse students—and with very different experiences and outcomes for students and teachers.

It is very difficult to imagine being appreciative in any way for much that the COVID-19 pandemic has done to our lives, yet it is forcing us to rethink some things we've long considered "givens" relative to our schools. Should we define schools as places with classrooms where teachers work with classes of twenty to thirty students of the same age to teach and learn the same prescribed materials in the same manner in the same time periods over the same 180-day school year? Should equality in our schools be measured by the provision of comparable services to all our students, and not by the learning outcomes realized for individual learners?

Yet long before and during the pandemic, all this has been very extensively discussed. Consider your own experiences in education and then reflect on the books and schools described in chapter 5, which concludes this book. Consider the following examples:

- "Suburban Public Schools Are Now Majority-Nonwhite," *Education Week*, Benjamin Herold, March 31, 2021, https://www.edweek.org/leadership/suburban-public-schools-are-now-majority-nonwhite-the-backlash-has-already-begun/2021/03.

- "What Parents Want: Education Preferences and Trade-Offs," The Thomas B. Fordham Institute, August 2013, https://fordhaminstitute.org/national/research/what-parents-want-education-preferences-and-trade-offs.
- "What Teens Want from Their Schools: A National Survey of High School Student Engagement," The Thomas B. Fordham Institute, June 2017. https://fordhaminstitute.org/national/research/what-teens-want-their-schools-national-survey-high-school-student-engagement.
- "School and the Tomato, Education Is No Longer a Monopoly," Bernie Bleske, February 28, 2019, https://medium.com/age-of-awareness/school-and-the-tomato-2e79605de6ac.
- "HISD Enrollment Down 4K amid Competition, District Turbulence," *Houston Chronicle*, Jacob Carpenter, November 2, 2018, https://www.houstonchronicle.com/news/education/article/HISD-enrollment-down-nearly-5K-amid-competition-13359347.php.

It is critical that we recognize how very different our students are today relative to those for whom our traditional schools were created generations ago. Figure 1.1 provides a table with statistics about enrollments for public school

District, City	Enrollment, Population	Student Demographics, Population Demographics					
		Af Am	Hisp	White	Am Ind	Asian	Other
Chicago Public Schools	355,156	35.90%	46.60%	10.80%	0.30%	4.20%	2.20%
City of Chicago	9,729,825	16.70%	22.10%	52.80%		6.40%	2.00%
Denver Public Schools	92,331	13.00%	56.00%	23.00%	1.00%	3.00%	4.00%
City of Denver	716,492	10.20%	31.80%	52.20%	1.40%	3.40%	
Houston School District	209,772	24.02%	61.84%	8.70%		4.05%	1.39%
City of Houston	2,099,451	23.15%	43.81%	25.62%		6.15%	1.28%
Los Angeles Unified School District	650,000	10.00%	73.40%	8.80%	0.04%	3.90%	3.86%
City of Los Angeles	3,797,576	9.60%	48.50%	28.70%		11.30%	1.90%
Miami-Dade County Public Schools	345,804	24.43%	63.49%	8.70%	0.09%	1.24%	2.05%
City of Miami	2,716,940	19.20%	70.00%	11.90%		1.00%	4.20%
New York City School System	1,126,501	25.50%	40.60%	15.10%		16.20%	2.60%
City of New York	8,336,817	25.50%	28.60%	33.30%	0.70%	12.70%	

Figure 1.1. Spreadsheet with data on cities, schools, and ethnic demographics by percentage. *Author created.*

systems in six very different municipalities across the country—Chicago, Denver, Houston, Los Angeles, Miami, and New York.

The data in figure 1.2 are based on census reports for Houston, Texas, from 1980, 1990, 2000, and 2010. What this shows is that the overall population of Houston is growing more rapidly, but the change varies by group. In 1980, there were 834,061 white residents, while in 2010, there were 537,901. The question is, has the number of whites declined over the entire metroplex or just in Houston? Is this a permanent change or will gentrification occur, with whites returning to Houston's inner-city areas to avoid long commutes and to access Houston's cultural assets?

- Chicago Public Schools, https://www.cps.edu/about/stats-facts.
- Denver Public Schools, https://en.wikipedia.org/wiki/Denver_Public_Schools.
- Houston ISD, https://www.houstonisd.org/Page/41879.
- Los Angeles Unified School District Students, https://laraec.net/los-angeles-unified-school-district.
- Miami-Dade County Public School Statistics/Demographics, http://publicschoolsk12.com/all-schools/fl/miami-dade-county.
- New York City Schools, https://www.schools.nyc.gov/about-us/reports/doe-data-at-a-glance.

The remarkable thing about the above statistics is the enormous demographic diversity in all of these school districts—that white students are a minority in every district, that there are big groups of students with different cultural and language backgrounds, and that these groups also have diverse family backgrounds and economic resources. And it seems quite improbable that any single approach to teaching and learning is going to serve all these students and communities sufficiently. Note that the percentage of white students in these public schools is less than the percentage of white residents in each of the cities listed. Are substantial numbers of white parents with the financial means opting to send their children to nonpublic schools such as private or charter schools?

Recognizing the similarities between these districts, this book draws upon its author's considerable background with Houston Independent School District (ISD) schools and has extracted illustrative statistics from the state (Texas Education Agency) and other sources for these explorations. However, this is *not* a book about Texas or the Houston ISD. The essential school and district characteristics considered, and the ideas proposed, are broadly applicable to other school districts in urban contexts across the country.

In 1967, the Texas legislature divided the state into twenty "regions" to assist school districts and charter schools in improving efficiencies and

City of Houston, Planning & Development Department
Race/Ethnicity: 1980-2010

Census	Race\Ethnicity	Population	Numerical Change	% Total
1980	White	834,061		52.3%
1980	Black/Af Am	436,392		27.4%
1980	Hispanic/Latino	281,331		17.6%
1980	Asian	34,259		2.1%
1980	Other	9,095		0.6%
1980	Total Population	1,595,138		100.0%
1990	White	662,766	(171,295)	40.6%
1990	Black/Af Am	448,148	11,756	27.5%
1990	Hispanic/Latino	450,556	169,225	27.6%
1990	Asian	66,993	32,734	4.1%
1990	Other	3,303	(5,792)	0.2%
1990	Total Population	1,631,766	36,628	100.0%
2000	White	601,851	(60,915)	30.8%
2000	Black/Af Am	487,851	39,703	25.0%
2000	Hispanic/Latino	730,865	280,309	37.4%
2000	Asian	106,620	39,627	5.5%
2000	Other	26,444	23,141	1.4%
2000	Total Population	1,953,631	321,865	100.0%
2010	White	537,901	(63,950)	25.6%
2010	Black/Af Am	485,956	(1,895)	23.1%
2010	Hispanic/Latino	919,668	188,803	43.8%
2010	Asian	129,098	22,478	6.1%
2010	Other	26,828	384	1.3%
2010	Total Population	2,099,451	145,820	100.0%

Race\Ethnicity	1980-2010 Population Change	% Change
White	(296,160)	-35.5%
Black/Af Am	49,564	11.4%
Hispanic/Latino	638,337	226.9%
Asian	94,839	276.8%
Other	17,733	195.0%
	504,313	

Figure 1.2. City of Houston changes in population and ethnicities by decade from 1980. *Author created.*

student performance. Below is information on the Region IV Education Service Center, of which HISD is the largest, central district—but there are numerous other significant districts with diverse schools and students. Region IV serves a seven-county area comprising forty-eight public school districts and thirty-nine open-enrollment charter schools, representing more than 1.2 million students, 99,000 educators, and 1,500 campuses.

The data in figure 1.3 and the text below describe the high schools in the Houston ISD and note the incredible diversity of their enrollments and the

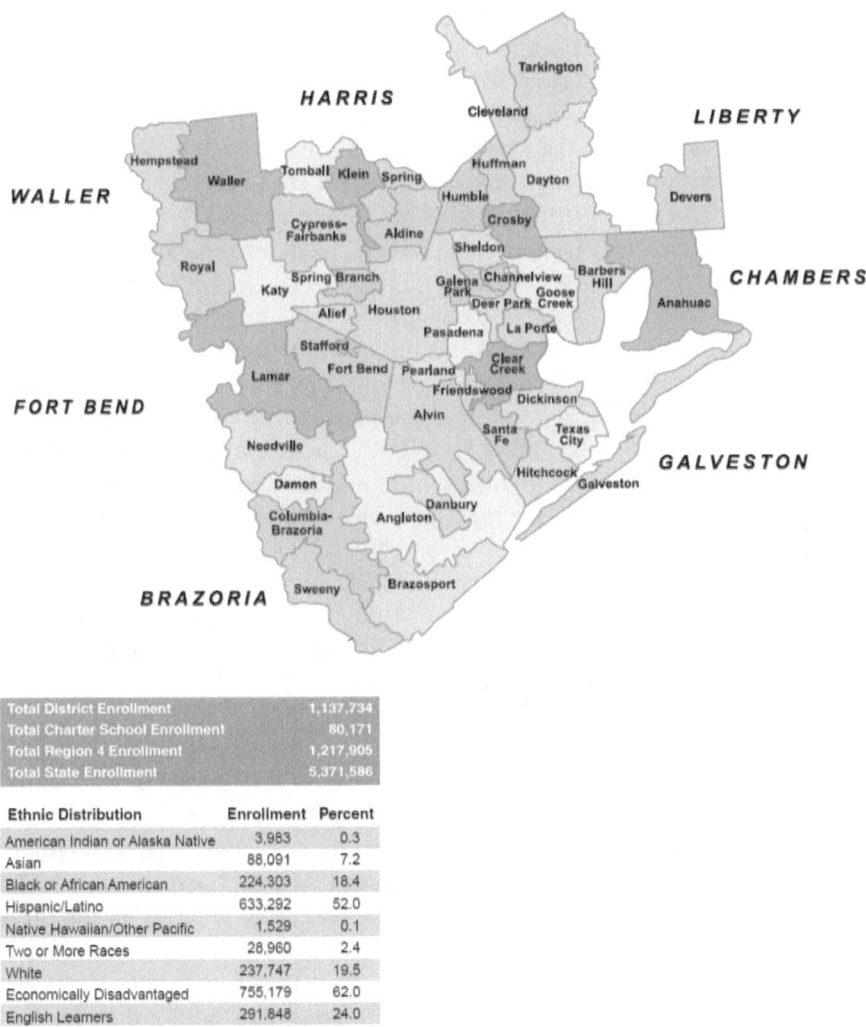

Total District Enrollment	1,137,734
Total Charter School Enrollment	80,171
Total Region 4 Enrollment	1,217,905
Total State Enrollment	5,371,586

Ethnic Distribution	Enrollment	Percent
American Indian or Alaska Native	3,983	0.3
Asian	88,091	7.2
Black or African American	224,303	18.4
Hispanic/Latino	633,292	52.0
Native Hawaiian/Other Pacific	1,529	0.1
Two or More Races	28,960	2.4
White	237,747	19.5
Economically Disadvantaged	755,179	62.0
English Learners	291,848	24.0

Figure 1.3. Diagrammatic map of the Region IV school districts. *Region IV Education Service Center, Houston, Texas*.

wide variety of outcomes they produce. Also in figure 1.3 is a map of the Houston ISD that shows via their Texas Education Agency (TEA) letter grades where the schools are located. The map's objective is to show that even with all its high schools, student choice is greatly constrained by the very long distances and travel times.

Furthermore, consider the Hechinger Report: the number of public school students could fall by more than 8 percent in a decade (https://hechingerreport.org/the-number-of-public-school-students-could-fall-by-more-than-8-in-a-decade) and the educational and financial implications of this decline. We not only need to improve the student outcomes realized but also create environments that attract both students and teachers.

We should reflect on Eric Klinenberg's book *Palaces for the People: How Social Infrastructure Can Help Fight Inequality, Polarization, and the Decline of Civic Life* and the idea that schools are essential parts of our communities—that they typically have big sites and could be much more lively, contributing, and participating parts of our communities. To delve even further into this, reflect on Stephen L. Klineberg's book *Prophetic City: Houston on the Cusp of a Changing America*.

We should note that, generally, our high schools are "islands" within the areas they serve—islands that are secured and isolated by fences, entrances with metal detectors and X-ray machines, and extensive athletic fields and parking. Are these schools working today, and will they continue to do so in the future? Will they be attractive to both teachers and students, and will they contribute to realizing good teaching and learning outcomes? Can we make our public high schools competitive with other schools seeking to serve our students?

Refer to the *Houston Chronicle* article "HISD Seeks Outside Help, Increased Advertising to Stop Enrollment Losses" (https://www.houstonchronicle.com/news/education/article/HISD-seeks-outside-help-increased-advertising-to-13683464.php) and refer to the next section.

TEXAS PUBLIC CHARTER SCHOOL FACTS

Since 1965 and the Immigration and Nationality Act, Houston's demographics have changed considerably. In 1980, the city was 52.3 percent white, 27.4 percent African American, and 17.6 percent Hispanic, whereas in the 2018 Houston Census, the population was 35 percent White, 17 percent African American, 37.6 percent Hispanic, and 7.8 percent Asian.

Concurrently, the distribution of these ethnic groups across the city also evolved. In earlier years, the more affluent chose to live in suburban areas out of concern about low-income and high-crime urban areas. But in more recent years, the costs and time of long commutes as well as the amenities of the inner city made life near the center of the city more attractive, and the resulting gentrification impacted property values and where different groups chose to live.

This was also reflected in HISD's 2018 enrollment, which was 9 percent white, 23 percent African American, 62 percent Hispanic, and 4.2 percent Asian (the remaining students were American Indian, Pacific Islanders, or persons of two or more races). The state identified 60.6 percent of students in Texas as economically disadvantaged, 19.5 percent as English learners, and 9.6 percent as special education students, whereas the school district identified 79.9 percent as economically disadvantaged, 31.8 percent as English learners, and 7.4 percent as special education students. The state's four-year longitudinal graduation rate is 90 percent, whereas it is 80.9 percent in the Houston School District.

The clear conclusion one might draw from these mind-numbing statistics is that HISD and the individual schools within the district have over the years served very different enrollments and that they are very likely to continue to do so for decades to come—this is not encouraging in terms of outcomes for future students.

These observations are extracted from several substantial scholarly publications:

- The 2020 Kinder Houston Area Survey, Rice/Kinder Institute for Urban Research, Steven L. Klineberg, https://kinder.rice.edu/houstonsurvey2020.
- "Big Texas Cities Are Rapidly Gentrifying, but None as Fast as Houston," Andy Olin, January 8, 2020, https://kinder.rice.edu/urbanedge/2020/01/08/biggest-texas-cities-are-gentrifying-quickly-and-fastest-gentrification-houston.
- "Gentrification Transforming Neighborhoods in Big Texas Cities," Southwest Economy, Fourth Quarter 2019, Yichen Su, https://www.dallasfed.org/research/swe/2019/swe1904/swe1904b.aspx.
- "America Is More Diverse than Ever, but Diversity Doesn't Equal Equality," Andy Olin, November 23, 2020, https://kinder.rice.edu/urbanedge/2020/11/23/america-racial-inequality-diversity-does-not-equal-equality.
- "Designing Schools for Human Flourishing & a Thriving Democracy," Erin Lynn Raab, PhD, https://erinraab.medium.com/designing-schools-for-human-flourishing-a-thriving-democracy-7db8a1eecc3b.

- "Inequality in Teaching and Schooling: How Opportunity Is Rationed to Students of Color in America," Linda Darling-Hammond, Stanford University School of Education, 2001, https://europepmc.org/books/n/nap10186/ddd00121/?extid=25057572.

Figures 1.4 and 1.5 were compiled from data assembled from the Texas Education Agency's 2017–2018 Texas Academic Performance Reports (https://tea.texas.gov/texas-schools/accountability/academic-accountability/performance-reporting/texas-academic-performance-reports), which provide comprehensive information for all the public schools in Texas.

These two figures provide data on HISD's thirty-eight high schools serving grades nine through twelve. The reports give each school a grade (ranging

HISD School		Enrollment Race/Ethnicity					Enrol by Student Group			Mobil.	Attend Rate	4 Yr Grad Rate	$/Student
Houston 2018 Census		17.0%	37.6%	35.5%		7.8%							
District		23.3%	62.0%	9.0%	0.2%	4.2%	79.9%	31.8%	7.4%	16.6%	95.4%	80.9	$9,726
State		12.6%	52.4%	27.8%	0.4%	4.4%	60.6%	19.5%	9.6%	15.4%	95.4%	90	$9,844
	No. Stds.	Af Am	Hisp	White	Am Ind	Asian	Econ Disadv	Eng Learn	Spec Ed			Campus	Campus
10 TEA A Grade 9-12 Schools, 5,660 Students, Avg 566													
Jones Futures Academy Mag	390	33.8%	64.4%	1.0%	0.5%	0.3%	90.3%	10.5%	9.0%	8.0%	96.7%	92.6%	$ 10,222
Challenge Early College	463	11.9%	72.1%	8.2%	0.4%	6.0%	76.0%	1.3%	0.9%	2.9%	97.4%	100.0%	$ 6,344
East Early College Chrtr	476	1.9%	94.3%	0.4%	0.2%	2.9%	88.2%	1.7%	0.0%	1.8%	97.4%	100.0%	$ 6,279
Eastwood Academy	432	1.4%	95.1%	1.4%	0.5%	1.4%	76.4%	3.2%	1.2%	1.6%	97.7%	100.0%	$ 7,255
Houston Acad Intl Chrtr	495	37.2%	52.9%	6.3%	0.2%	2.4%	66.5%	1.2%	0.8%	2.9%	95.2%	99.1%	$ 5,965
N Houston Early Coll Chrtr	484	7.6%	90.7%	0.6%	0.0%	1.0%	84.9%	6.4%	0.9%	2.3%	97.6%	100.0%	$ 6,768
Carnegie Vanguard	808	10.5%	32.1%	23.3%	0.2%	30.4%	31.3%	0.2%	0.5%	3.0%	97.6%	98.6%	$ 6,655
Debakey Health Prof Chrtr	891	16.3%	35.9%	12.2%	0.8%	33.0%	44.3%	0.6%	1.7%	4.6%	98.2%	98.4%	$ 12,747
HS Law, Justice Magnet	469	20.3%	75.9%	3.2%	0.0%	0.2%	82.5%	1.5%	1.5%	5.9%	95.7%	100.0%	$ 9,056
Kinder HSPVA Mag	752	17.3%	26.3%	43.9%	0.5%	8.4%	17.8%	0.1%	0.8%	0.9%	96.6%	99.5%	$ 7,838
A Schools Averages		15.8%	64.0%	10.1%	0.3%	8.6%	65.8%	2.7%	1.7%	3.4%	97.0%	98.8%	$ 7,913
9 TEA B Grade 9-12 Schools, 13,282 Students, Avg 1476													
Energized for STEM SE Chrtr	315	13.0%	86.3%	0.3%	0.0%	0.3%	97.5%	49.5%	2.5%	9.7%	97.2%	87.0%	$ 9,988
Energized for STEM WH Chrtr	200	2.5%	97.5%	0.0%	0.0%	0.0%	100.0%	59.5%	1.5%	6.9%	98.0%	97.4%	$ 7,907
Mount Carmel Academy Chrtr	340	9.1%	87.4%	2.6%	0.0%	0.9%	72.4%	7.9%	2.4%	4.5%	96.2%	97.6%	$ 7,753
Bellaire	3,307	20.1%	42.1%	22.1%	0.2%	13.3%	48.7%	11.0%	6.7%	9.8%	94.2%	92.2%	$ 7,000
Energy Institute High Mag	764	25.3%	55.1%	14.3%	0.8%	3.8%	56.3%	4.1%	5.6%	4.1%	96.2%		$ 6,846
Lamar IB Prog	3,082	29.8%	35.6%	26.7%	0.4%	5.6%	45.5%	4.8%	5.3%	8.3%	94.3%	93.8%	$ 6,928
KIPP Houston Chrtr	676	17.0%	79.6%	0.4%	0.3%	2.4%	84.9%	6.4%	0.8%	2.3%	97.6%		
Westside	2,897	28.9%	43.1%	19.0%	0.1%	7.2%	56.9%	9.5%	6.3%	12.5%	95.0%	90.9%	$ 7,105
Heights HS	2,377	10.9%	78.7%	8.3%	0.4%	1.1%	69.8%	4.5%	7.2%	6.6%	95.2%	96.5%	$ 7,428
B Schools Averages		17.4%	67.3%	10.4%	0.2%	3.8%	70.2%	17.5%	4.3%	7.2%	96.0%	93.6%	$ 9,018

Figure 1.4. TEA high school statistics: A and B grade schools. *Author created from data assembled from the Texas Education Agency's 2017–2018 Texas Academic Performance Reports (https://tea.texas.gov/texas-schools/accountability/academic-accountability/performance-reporting/texas-academic-performance-reports), which provide comprehensive information for all the public schools in Texas.*

Our Evolving Cities and Schools 9

HISD School	Enrollment Race/Ethnicity					Enrol by Student Group			Mobil.	Attend Rate	4 Yr Grad Rate	$/Student
Houston 2018 Census	17.0%	37.6%	35.5%		7.8%							
District	23.3%	62.0%	9.0%	0.2%	4.2%	79.9%	31.8%	7.4%	16.6%	95.4%	80.9	$9,726
State	12.6%	52.4%	27.8%	0.4%	4.4%	60.6%	19.5%	9.6%	15.4%	95.4%	90	$9,844
	No. Stds.	Af Am	Hisp	White	Am Ind	Asian	Econ Disadv	Eng Learn	Spec Ed			Campus	Campus
16 TEA C High 9-12 Schools, 25,899 Students, Avg 1619												
Milby HS	1903	4.5%	94.2%	0.8%	0.1%	0.4%	92.6%	18.8%	9.9%	16.5%	91.3%	77.3%	$ 7,649
Chavez	2,682	9.0%	85.7%	1.0%	0.0%	4.1%	87.5%	16.8%	7.7%	14.0%	90.5%	77.4%	$ 7,183
Northside HS	1,540	14.3%	84.4%	0.8%	0.2%	0.2%	93.8%	19.2%	10.3%	15.8%	90.7%	81.2%	$ 8,135
Westbury HS	2,341	33.1%	62.0%	2.1%	0.2%	1.7%	93.2%	24.1%	10.9%	19.3%	92.9%	83.1%	$ 7,446
Worthing Mag	781	74.4%	23.6%	1.4%	0.0%	0.5%	99.9%	10.5%	20.0%	33.6%	90.2%	65.8%	$ 9,614
Austin	1,685	9.0%	89.5%	0.9%	0.2%	0.1%	93.2%	25.7%	11.6%	17.6%	91.8%	86.1%	$ 7,649
Kashmere	777	64.2%	33.3%	1.4%	0.4%	0.0%	97.7%	13.8%	17.8%	31.0%	88.4%	67.2%	$ 10,867
Madison	1,736	38.4%	59.6%	0.6%	0.3%	0.5%	76.9%	21.4%	12.4%	23.4%	88.5%	71.4%	$ 7,894
Scarborough Futures Acad	752	19.1%	75.9%	3.3%	0.1%	0.7%	92.2%	24.6%	12.4%	20.2%	93.5%	88.8%	$ 8,615
Waltrip Research Tech Mag	1,902	14.0%	76.8%	7.7%	0.4%	0.4%	67.2%	15.3%	9.8%	13.0%	93.8%	81.1%	$ 6,926
Furr	1,035	16.8%	80.8%	1.3%	0.2%	0.6%	94.0%	21.8%	11.4%	19.9%	87.8%	72.5%	$ 8,640
Booker T Washington HS	758	47.2%	49.2%	2.2%	0.4%	0.0%	94.6%	17.2%	14.0%	31.5%	89.0%	64.6%	$ 9,086
Houston Math Science Tech	2,612	8.4%	89.4%	2.0%	0.1%	0.1%	95.6%	28.0%	11.9%	18.5%	93.2%	90.0%	$ 7,039
Sharpstown High	1,689	19.9%	74.7%	1.8%	0.4%	3.0%	95.8%	47.5%	9.3%	23.6%	90.7%	73.3%	$ 7,938
Sterling High Aviation	1,483	49.3%	48.0%	1.7%	0.3%	0.3%	95.7%	15.4%	0.15	27.7%	90.3%	73.9%	$ 7,781
Wisdom	2,023	14.5%	74.6%	5.1%	0.3%	5.1%	99.0%	56.0%	7.6%	22.5%	94.3%	66.4%	$ 7,253
C Schools Averages		27.3%	68.9%	2.1%	0.2%	1.1%	91.8%	23.5%	12.0%	21.8%	91.1%	76.3%	$ 8,107
2 TEA D Grade 9-12 Schools, 1,867 Students, Avg 934												
North Forest High	993	61.3%	37.1%	0.9%	0.4%	0.0%	91.7%	10.7%	12.2%	27.9%	89.9%	77.8%	$ 9,128
Yates	874	87.2%	10.9%	0.8%	2.0%	0.3%	81.8%	4.3%	18.6%	28.6%	89.3%	65.9%	$ 9,574
D Schools Averages		74.3%	24.0%	0.9%	1.2%	0.2%	86.8%	7.5%	15.4%	28.3%	89.6%	71.9%	$ 9,351
1 TEA F Grade 9-12 School, 873 Students												
Wheatley	873	52.7%	46.2%	0.3%	0.0%	0.3%	93.8%	15.9%	20.5%	28.5%	87.5%	66.2%	$ 9,387
D Schools Averages		52.7%	46.2%	0.3%	0.0%	0.3%	93.8%	15.9%	20.5%	28.5%	87.5%	66.2%	$ 9,387
38 Schools		Af Am	Hisp	White	Am Ind	Asian	Econ Disadv	Eng Learn	Spec Ed	Mobil.	Attend Rate	Grd Rate	$/Student
All Schools Averages		25.1%	64.2%	6.1%	0.3%	3.7%	79.6%	15.6%	7.9%	14.0%	93.6%	80.9%	$ 8,051

Figure 1.5. TEA high school statistics: C, D, and F grade schools. *Author created from data assembled from the Texas Education Agency's 2017–2018 Texas Academic Performance Reports (https://tea.texas.gov/texas-schools/accountability/academic-accountability/performance-reporting/texas-academic-performance-reports), which provide comprehensive information for all the public schools in Texas.*

from A to F), and the figures group HISD's schools by these grades. The A and B schools are listed in figure 1.4, and the C, D, and F schools are listed in figure 1.5. At the end of each grade group, there are averages for all the stats to facilitate comparison. Across the top of the tables, there are both Houston census and overall HISD numbers for all their schools for comparison purposes.

A brief description of the information is provided immediately below, and then following the figures are analytical observations extracted from the data.

- HISD schools: The first two columns identify the schools, the nature of their academic programs (comprehensive school, magnet school, or charter school), and their enrollment.
- Enrollment race/ethnicity: These five columns describe the nature of the schools' enrollments. In each of the columns, the dark gray cells identify the school(s) with the highest percentage, and the light gray cells identify the one(s) with the lowest percentage.
- Enrollment by student group: These three columns list the percentages of the schools' enrollment that are economically disadvantaged, English learners, or special education students—and those with high mobility rates (who relocate and change schools during the academic year), and the overall attendance rates for the schools.
- Four-year graduation rate: This column notes the percentage of the students who complete the learning requirements in four years.
- $/student: This notes the annual expenditures at each school per student enrolled, which includes the costs related to students who did and who did not graduate. The costs also vary between the schools depending on the instructional and extracurricular programs they offer.

At the end of the chart in figure 1.5, there are averages for all of the HISD high schools.

The ten A schools serve 5,660 students (average 566/campus), and most are magnets or charters with strong academic focuses. The nine B schools serve 13,282 students (average 1,476/campus) and include the district's two largest comprehensive high schools (3,307 and 3,082), with the lowest percentages of economically disadvantaged students. The sixteen C schools serve a total of 25,899 students (average 1,619/campus), and most are traditional comprehensive schools. The two D schools serve a total of 1,867 students, and the one F school serves 873 students.

Hispanic students comprise the largest percentage of enrollment in the A, B, and C groups of schools—but African American students are the largest groups in the D and F schools. Of the total students in the HISD high schools, 25.1 percent are African American, 64.2 percent are Hispanic, 6.1 percent are white, 0.3 percent are American Indian, and 3.7 percent are Asian.

Student mobility is low in the A and B schools, but much higher in the others. The percentage of economically disadvantaged students is considerable in the A (65.8 percent) and B (70.2 percent) schools, and very high in the C, D, and F schools.

The percentages of African American and Hispanic students in HISD are considerably larger than those in the city census (see the text at the top of either chart). In contrast, the percentages for white and Asian students are smaller in the district than in the city census. Are white and Asian families who can afford it electing to send their students to private schools instead of HISD and charter schools? What are the long-term implications of this? How can HISD attract a more representative cross-section of students?

On average, the majority of students in each school group are first Hispanic and second African American. White and Asian percentages are much smaller and well below the percentages in the overall Houston census.

The economically disadvantaged students in the A schools graduate at a much higher rate than those in the lower-grade schools. How can the varied success rates for these students in the different schools be explained?

The cost/student is lower for the A grade schools and higher for the F grade schools. The cost/graduate (the cost/student divided by the percentage of graduates) is much lower for the A schools than the C, D, and F schools. If we measured costs based on student outcomes, would low-performing schools be acceptable to parents and taxpayers?

Needless to say, assembling all these data and writing this book took a serious amount of time, and it was surprising and worrisome in September 2020 to find that the list of HISD's high schools further evolved, as a few schools were closed or merged with other schools, or entirely new schools were created. But, reflecting on all this, it was noted that the diversity of the students served had not diminished at all and that the giant question coming from all these statistics has, if anything, only grown: How can we make schools that will raise the bar for all of HISD's diverse students and communities?

Figure 1.6 provides a map of HISD, which serves 214,175 students (as of 2020) in an area of 312 square miles. The objective of the map is to show that the students served are incredibly diverse and spread out over a large area. There may be schools somewhere in the district that meet most students' needs—but the students and schools are so spread out that it is impossible to easily connect them all with cars, buses, and public transit. What are different ways to make teaching and learning work to serve such huge areas? Houston may be a remarkable example, but its large size, low density, and diverse demographics are not unique.

While the data above focus on the Houston ISD as an illustrative example, the two publications below clearly note that the diversity of its students and outcomes are not at all limited to Houston.

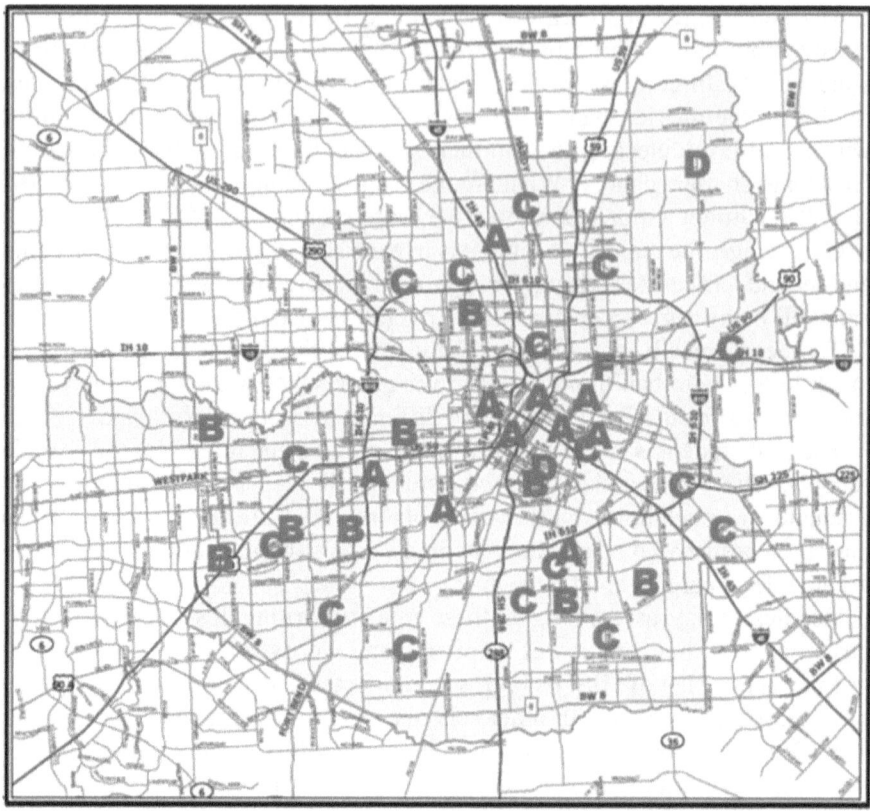

Figure 1.6. HISD map showing locations of high schools with TEA performance grades. *The base map has been developed by the City of Houston's Planning and Development Department. The author has inserted the HISD academic performance grades.*

- "America Is More Diverse than Ever, but Diversity Doesn't Equal Equality," Andy Olin, November 23, 2020, https://kinder.rice.edu/urbanedge/2020/11/23/america-racial-inequality-diversity-does-not-equal-equality.
- "Inequality in Teaching and Schooling: How Opportunity Is Rationed to Students of Color in America," Linda Darling-Hammond, Stanford University School of Education, 2001, https://europepmc.org/books/n/nap10186/ddd00121/?extid=25057572&src=med&fid=ddd00124.

Reflect on your own experiences in education:

- Are your schools and the students they serve as diverse as those in the Houston ISD? Are the outcomes for your school's students comparably diverse?

- What is fair for the students in your school and/or district? Comparable facilities, teachers, and expenditures? Or comparable outcomes for students? How do you measure success for medical services? For educational services?
- Is the diversity of outcomes acceptable for your students and parents? What about for the communities in your district? Is that OK for taxpayers? Is it OK for preparing the district's future citizens? Is it OK for employers and the people they will need in the future?

Chapter 2

Schools for the Future

Instruction, Technology, Time, Spaces, Community, Funding

The objectives here are to begin by reflecting on the Elements of Schooling concept, which describes how the various parts of our schools work together to shape the environment for teaching and learning—and then to explore our traditional schools via the same concepts in an effort to anticipate how they will serve teachers and students in the future we envision at this date. The Elements of Schooling were first briefly described in the introduction to the book *Learning without Classrooms* (Frank Kelly and Ted McCain, 3–5).

The diagram in figure 2.1 is a brief analysis of our current, traditional schools that provides a base from which to consider the future. Another edition of the diagram follows in figure 2.2 as an introduction to a concept for preserving and transforming our schools to realize powerful aspirations for the future.

The school environment is shaped by six elements:

- Instructional approach: How do teachers and students work with each other to realize learning?
- Technology resources: What is the nature of the materials with which teachers and students communicate? Books? Marker boards? Lectures? Videos? Digital resources? Online materials? Computers? Individual devices? Online resources?
- Use of time: How is time organized to accommodate teaching, learning, facilities, and the use of funds?
- Community context: How does the school relate to the community in which it is located and which it serves? How do the school and community benefit each other?

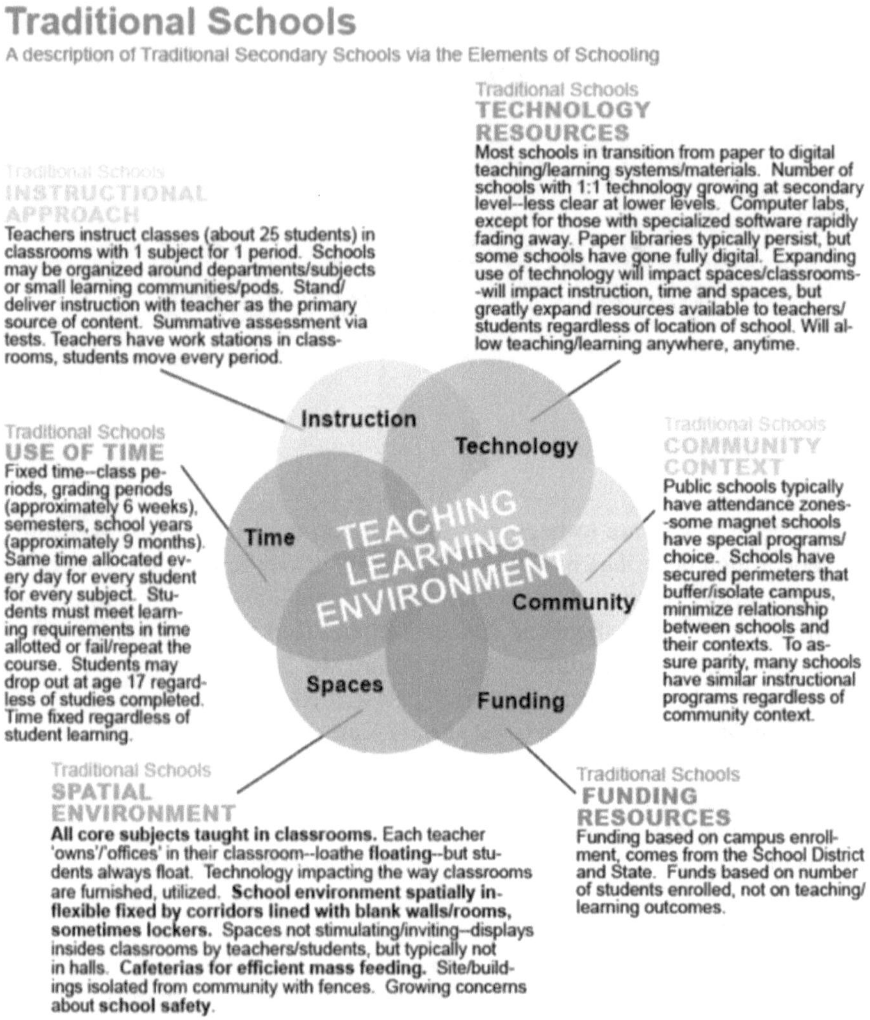
Traditional Schools
A description of Traditional Secondary Schools via the Elements of Schooling
Traditional Schools
TECHNOLOGY RESOURCES
Most schools in transition from paper to digital teaching/learning systems/materials. Number of schools with 1:1 technology growing at secondary level--less clear at lower levels. Computer labs, except for those with specialized software rapidly fading away. Paper libraries typically persist, but some schools have gone fully digital. Expanding use of technology will impact spaces/classrooms--will impact instruction, time and spaces, but greatly expand resources available to teachers/students regardless of location of school. Will allow teaching/learning anywhere, anytime.
Traditional Schools
INSTRUCTIONAL APPROACH
Teachers instruct classes (about 25 students) in classrooms with 1 subject for 1 period. Schools may be organized around departments/subjects or small learning communities/pods. Stand/deliver instruction with teacher as the primary source of content. Summative assessment via tests. Teachers have work stations in classrooms, students move every period.
Instruction
Technology
Time
TEACHING LEARNING ENVIRONMENT
Community
Spaces
Funding
Traditional Schools
USE OF TIME
Fixed time--class periods, grading periods (approximately 6 weeks), semesters, school years (approximately 9 months). Same time allocated every day for every student for every subject. Students must meet learning requirements in time allotted or fail/repeat the course. Students may drop out at age 17 regardless of studies completed. Time fixed regardless of student learning.
Traditional Schools
COMMUNITY CONTEXT
Public schools typically have attendance zones--some magnet schools have special programs/choice. Schools have secured perimeters that buffer/isolate campus, minimize relationship between schools and their contexts. To assure parity, many schools have similar instructional programs regardless of community context.
Traditional Schools
SPATIAL ENVIRONMENT
All core subjects taught in classrooms. Each teacher 'owns'/'offices' in their classroom--loathe floating--but students always float. Technology impacting the way classrooms are furnished, utilized. School environment spatially inflexible fixed by corridors lined with blank walls/rooms, sometimes lockers. Spaces not stimulating/inviting--displays insides classrooms by teachers/students, but typically not in halls. Cafeterias for efficient mass feeding. Site/buildings isolated from community with fences. Growing concerns about school safety.
Traditional Schools
FUNDING RESOURCES
Funding based on campus enrollment, comes from the School District and State. Funds based on number of students enrolled, not on teaching/learning outcomes.

Figure 2.1. Diagram of six Elements of Schooling describing traditional schools. ***Author created.***

- Spatial environment: How do the school's spaces contribute to or constrain teaching and learning objectives?
- Funding resources: Are the funds available sufficient to realize the teaching and learning objectives and community aspirations? Is the school using its teachers, technology, and facilities to realize the school's objectives economically?

PORTAL Schools
Teaching, Learning for a Diverse World

PORTAL Schools
INSTRUCTIONAL APPROACH
Instruction in all core subjects comes to individual students wherever/whenever via 1:1 technology. Students have primary responsibility for pursuing digital learning. Teachers have dual role--as **teachers** in their area of expertise, to guide/monitor/support individual students on line, and in individual and small group face to face processes as appropriate--and as **advisors** to a multiage group of students about their overall academic lives for the duration of their time at the school. Group instruction is used for performing arts, some CTE, physical education/athletic areas in which group activities and specialized spaces/equipment are necessary. Students/teachers have access via the net to the world's resources, libraries.

PORTAL Schools
USE OF TIME
Schooling is a continuous service with no periods/bells, semesters or years. Within prerequisites defined by the school, students start courses when ready, and finish when they've realized stipulated outcomes. Students and teachers meet when helpful to support learning. Both students and teachers work with the school to define what they will do and when so that the school may plan the efficient use of staff and facilities. For students, minimum levels of study are prescribed by truancy laws, but students may complete studies in more/less than the traditional 4 years. Teachers may teach more or less than the traditional 9 month school year, earn more or less, accommodate diverse family needs.

PORTAL Schools
TECHNOLOGY RESOURCES
Every teacher and student has a personal digital device linked to their school's network and the world. Students are closely linked to their teachers and advisors, and to each other--and to vast resources both within and beyond the school. Schools of every size and location, have digital libraries with online access to the world's great libraries. Serving as research teachers, librarians help students learn to access/use the net to enhance their studies. The school has spaces for specialized equipment for science, projects/presentations, specialized graphics/videos, etc.

PORTAL Schools
COMMUNITY CONTEXT
Common areas within the school are linked to the community/world of which it is a part with live constantly changing digital displays that inform, stimulate students and teachers. The objective is to expose/inform students and faculty about local and world events and resources, and to help students imagine their own possibilities/futures--and to give meaning to their studies and the pace of their learning/work.

PORTAL Schools
FUNDING RESOURCES
Fund schools, and measure the cost of schooling, on the basis of learning realized vs. instruction delivered. Describe school costs on the basis of cost/credits earned/outcomes realized, not the costs per student/classes taught. Utilize staff and facilities continuously and efficiently all year to support/realize learning. Measure how fair school funding is among diverse campuses and districts by considering outcomes for students vs. $$$/student.

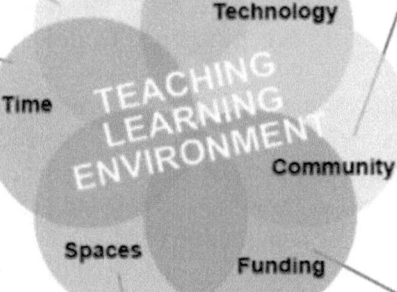

PORTAL Schools
SPATIAL ENVIRONMENT
Portal schools may be created within modified existing secondary schools. Students and teachers have individual workstations grouped in multi-grade level advisories. Students work in the same space with the same advisor and an evolving group of colleagues throughout their time on the campus. Advisories are clearly defined, but ideally are visually open--so that everyone has a sense of the life in the school. Students usually work on campus, but with the approval of their family and advisor, may at times work at home and off campus.

Figure 2.2. Diagram of six Elements of Schooling describing portal schools. *Author created.*

We must recognize that the Elements of Schooling are integrally related—that we cannot alter any one of them without impacting, and being impacted by, the others. Some illustrative examples:

- The agrarian calendar and teacher lectures have shaped our education programs at every level for generations. If teachers' lectures are the primary source of content, then schools need to assemble students in proper spaces on a reliable schedule. Furthermore, a school cannot deviate from this schedule without impacting large numbers of teachers and students, and the need to reschedule teaching and learning, and that impacts facilities and funding.
- Most recently, consider the coronavirus that shut down schools early in the 2020 spring semester and may not open until the fall of 2021. As this was written in the fall of 2021, it is not at all clear how the teaching and learning lost during the last and current school year will be recovered, nor what will happen to assure that the coming school year will be complete. Rigid school time is impacting teaching and learning. Schools have tried to use digital homeschooling, but that was the first attempt at this at such a scale. Furthermore, all of this has enormous cost implications in terms of staff, technology, and facilities.

So, we hope that in reading all that follows regarding our existing schools and concepts for schools in the future, you will consider each idea and your own thoughts within the Elements of Schooling context.

We must reflect here on how large cities and school districts with great and evolving diversities of communities and students can provide education services that are effective and fair to all. Traditionally, most major school districts are comprised of multiple elementary and secondary schools related to attendance zones, each offering comparable full education programs and facilities for their students. Today these offerings are complemented by magnet programs and charter schools.

But in some major cities, the demographics, languages, and economics of students and their families vary enormously, and the overall district-wide student outcomes are quite diverse, with a substantial number of schools failing to help their students obtain the learning they need for their futures (see chapter 1).

The option of allowing students to select their school might benefit some students and schools, but in very large districts in large urban areas, those options are greatly diminished by long distances, time, and the cost challenges of attending distant schools. The objective is to explore how today's schools and their technology could be integrated to realize better teaching and learning outcomes district wide.

In Houston, the state's Texas Education Agency (TEA) has been very concerned for some time about the school board "squabbling" and their failure to "end a cycle of low performance," which has "paved the way for state takeover" of the district. Among the challenges the TEA noted are:

- a cluster of perpetually struggling schools
- a destructive legacy of segregation and racism
- a student population in which about 80 percent are economically disadvantaged
- many students who are immigrants with limited English skills
- high teacher and principal turnover at low-performing schools

However, HISD is "still home to some of the nation's best schools," and the "district has an overall B rating." "However, 21 of HISD's 280 campuses received failing grades from the State this year, including Wheatley High School, whose seventh consecutive failure triggered state law requiring TEA to either close the school or install a board of managers."

The point here is that HISD has serious problems that the *Houston Chronicle* explored in four editorials (see below) in December 2019. The quotations above are from those publications.

- "Time for Radical Improvement: A State Takeover Must Lead to Lasting Changes at Struggling Houston ISD," *Houston Chronicle*, December 26, 2019, https://www.houstonchronicle.com/opinion/editorials/article/HISD-in-crisis-Looming-state-takeover-presents-14929858.php.
- "HISD at a Crossroads: Learning from Others, and Our Own Past," editorial, *Houston Chronicle*, Editorial Board, December 27, 2019, updated December 30, 2019, https://www.houstonchronicle.com/opinion/editorials/article/HISD-at-a-crossroads-Learning-from-others-and-14933039.php.
- "Road Map to Transformation: HISD Has Strengths to Build on but a Long Way to Go to Get the Results Its Students Deserve," *Houston Chronicle*, Sunday edition, Editorial Board, December 29, 2019, https://www.pressreader.com/usa/houston-chronicle-sunday/20191229/281895890158785.
- "HISD at a Crossroads: A Call to All Houstonians to participate," editorial, *Houston Chronicle*, December 30, 2019, updated December 30, 2019, https://www.houstonchronicle.com/opinion/editorials/article/HISD-at-a-crossroads-A-call-to-all-Houstonians-14934929.php.

However, all the editorials and political discussions keep mentioning replacing some or all of the board or some teachers, and drawing on "best practices" from other cities and school districts. Replacing board members and/or teachers would accomplish *almost nothing*—and would be much more of a disruption than a solution. The real question is, does HISD have a staff problem? Or a problem with the nature of the schools serving its students, communities, and city at this date? Moreover, will the problems only get worse if they simply try to tweak the current schools?

Garrett Reed, a dedicated, lively teacher at Wisdom High School (Houston ISD) who wrote an op-ed for the *Houston Chronicle* (https://www.houstonchronicle.com/opinion/outlook/article/Children-at-Risk-gave-my-school-an-F-They-were-14291266.php), was both right and wrong about his criticism of Children at Risk and their statistics about schools and his school in particular. He was right that he and other teachers at Wisdom are doing remarkable things for the school's astonishingly diverse students—students who speak more than fifty different languages.

However, despite all this, their students' overall learning is still not sufficient or comparable to that in some other HISD schools. This lack of success is what the Children at Risk analysis reflected. We need to give the Garrett Reeds and their students in HISD a better opportunity to do the super job and realize the excellent outcomes to which they aspire. (See the tables in figures 1.4 and 1.5 with statistics about HISD high schools.)

Individual teachers are *not* the issue; rather it is the schools that are the problem—meaning how we teach, the instructional materials and technology we employ, the way we use and organize time, the spaces we have, and the way we use funds—because they were not designed and are not operated to serve diverse students and communities across such a huge district and/or city.

And we, the public, are part of the problem because we've not been seriously concerned about how poorly many of our students are faring in our schools—and we've blamed the students and their communities. Over time and across the large area of our city, we have created magnet schools to offer varied programs, but not planned them with the intent or capacity to serve the whole district and diverse students—but rather to provide very exceptional focused studies for small numbers of students in narrow areas—Debakey/medicine, HSPVA/performing and visual arts, etc.

We have realized parity of core studies, funding, staffing, and facilities, but failed to realize what really counts—parity of student learning. The challenge here is agreeing on what "student learning" means and how to measure it.

Diane Ravitch's *Slaying Goliath: The Passionate Resistance to Privatization and the Fight to Save America's Public Schools* (2020) provides very substantial and current background on the status of our schools and why we should be very concerned whether they can serve our students. Extend into the future some of the funding and educational issues she raises, and it is not hard to imagine our public schools in many school districts failing both economically and educationally.

Referring to the TEA data chart on Houston high schools in figures 1.4 and 1.5, how can a district like HISD, or those it serves, live with having thirty-eight high schools (grades nine through twelve, 47,581 students) of which nineteen are schools enrolling 18,942 students and getting A or B ratings and nineteen are schools enrolling 28,639 students and getting C, D, or F ratings? Please remember that we are using Houston ISD only as a representative example of a district with diverse students. We could have worked with other large metroplexes as examples and explored very similar issues.

How can HISD have wonderful magnet schools that serve tiny enrollments knowing that they can't possibly serve all the students who might find them of great interest, and knowing that even if they could, how would students get to and from them across the huge city with its congested traffic and minimal public transit? How do students and parents learn about the large range of magnet programs—and how do students envision what they want to study and make informed choices?

We might consider Erin Lynn Raab's "The Four Purposes of Schooling" (February 14, 2018, https://medium.com/reenvisioned/f-efficiency-in-education-organize-schooling-for-possibility-70c6cbc31bc0). She noted that "the first step toward shifting a system is knowing what it's meant to do" and asked "how can we reimagine school?" without asking "why do we have school?" She said there are four distinct purposes for schooling:

- Individual possibility—classic education shaping the learning and development of individual students.
- Social possibility—socialization processes shaping collective culture and social norms at the community, national, and global levels.
- Social efficiency—the classic human-capital perspective, to sustain current social, economic, and political institutions.
- Individual efficiency—to serve an individual's own ability to navigate the education or socioeconomic systems, often termed "social mobility."

Raab observed that these four purposes are applicable to every society that maintains a school system—then noted that we must "shift out of the efficiency frames and into possibility frames when we design school practice or policies." And she asked two huge questions:

- "How do we design environments in which students' core needs are met so they are able to learn and grow?"
- "How do we create experiences that give children opportunities to practice the capabilities, mindsets, and character they need to be agentive citizens who are able to work with others to make a better world?"

A question: Is a high school a place organized around teachers in specific subjects working with classes of approximately twenty-five students in fixed classroom spaces with fixed instructional materials on fixed schedules within a fixed school year?

A proposal: Could a high school be an assembly of teaching and learning services and resources that has no set address or, alternatively, has multiple addresses/campuses, with some specialized spaces for teaching and learning, and has no set teaching/learning schedules over the whole calendar year, where schooling is a continuous service and invites students and teachers to work in multiple places in multiple ways on multiple schedules with multiple digital resources to realize all sorts of good, diverse learning outcomes?

- Could we make the entire HISD group of senior high schools into a single "school" that has multiple campuses—but which collectively have the ability with today's digital technology to serve every student's individual needs? Where Wisdom and Wheatley students have access to exactly the same instruction and learning materials and faculty as those in DeBakey, Eastwood, Carnegie, Lamar, Bellaire, etc.?

  And where every student has the face-to-face and online supervision of, guidance by, and support and encouragement of, and is informed and stimulated by, and is well known by, an advisor/teacher who tailors the process to them individually, and who sticks with them and their family for their entire time at the "school" through graduation? Be very clear, though this is not the "homeschooling" pursued during the coronavirus lockdown, digital technology is still very important.

- Could the existing individual campuses be perceived as, and function as, not separate schools, but rather as "portals" through which students access all the education services and faculty, and teaching and learning resources and opportunities, the district provides—and let students, parents, and advisors/teachers formulate from this the optimum resources and approach for each student?

  Could teachers, working individually or in groups, create their own materials best suited for the students they know, or could teachers draw from instructional material sources similar to those the Rice faculty created in their OpenStax and Connexions programs? The teaching materials should be vast and readily available—and grow continuously and enormously over time.

- Would the huge disparities between the nature of the enrollments in HISD's current secondary schools matter if there were no attendance zones and there was one HISD high school with multiple campuses (like the Methodist and Memorial Hermann Hospital Groups, for example)—and each campus was, among other things, a "home base" for a group of students and teachers where each has their own place to work?

- How much more engaging, enjoyable, and effective would it be for students (and their parents and teachers) to go to a school attuned to their needs and dedicated to good outcomes for them? A place where they really want to be? Schools could do a dramatically better job of "selling themselves" to prospective students and parents.

  In huge urban districts like Houston ISD (as opposed to magnets, charters, and private schools), how many school websites are truly clear about how teaching and learning work at their school—the intent/spirit of the whole environment—and how its graduates have done beyond high school? How many high school corridors are enlivened with displays about the world and news, about professions, about universities—about things of interest to students and their futures?

There follows a detailed description and analysis via the Elements of Schooling for the proposed portal school.

INSTRUCTION

Shape schooling to individual backgrounds, capabilities, interests, and learning styles. Treat individual learners more like patients in a doctor's care or hospital, and less like a student in Ms. Smith's tenth-grade, third-period, fall semester English class. Students should not be sorted by our perceptions of their competencies—rather, schools should support, help, guide, encourage, and push each student to succeed. We should intentionally, actively engage each student in shaping and realizing their own learning.

"The truth is that you cannot manufacture students any more than you can manufacture a tomato." "Schooling is more like gardening than manufacturing." And in today's cities, we must make schools to grow an incredible diversity of "tomatoes" ("Please Stop Trying to Manufacture Students!," Erin Lynn Raab, https://medium.com/age-of-awareness/please-stop-trying-to-manufacture-students-623492e60134).

Before each student starts at the school, the student and his or her parents must have serious substantial discussions with a representative of the overall district/school, as well as with the teacher/advisor with whom they are to work, to explore in depth the student's/family's background, the student's previous school experiences and transcript/portfolio, and their interests and aspirations for both the immediate and long-term future.

The student and family should be advised well in advance about the nature of the discussion to be held, and they must come prepared. As the student progresses in his or her learning, the group should hold similar discussions at least annually to review how the student is progressing and to identify what needs to be modified.

Faculty have dual roles in portal schools—they function as teachers in their area of expertise by guiding, informing, and monitoring students in their online studies, but they do little or no live lectures, and they function as advisors who counsel the small group of multi-age students in their advisory throughout their life in the school.

In this dual role, they guide both students and parents along individual paths based on their individual learning interests and needs. They are a source of support available to students throughout their entire time at the school. As advisors, teachers help students (and parents) navigate the vast resources available through the portal.

The workload of teachers/advisors is carefully monitored over time to be certain that they have the time and opportunity to respond to the diverse academic and personal needs of their students. The ProUnitas (https://www.prounitas.org) program can help facilitate this process.

Provide, for every student, individualized schooling geared to his/her capabilities, interests, and learning styles. Recognize the diversity (ethnicities, languages,[1] incomes, home environments) of the students and draw upon the school's huge teaching and learning resources and flexible time to help students succeed in diverse ways. Traditional schools are geared to mass instruction, with very little individualized/flexible instruction, learning materials, or time—the industrial approach.

If in factories some "products" are defective, we discard them. But the "products" of our traditional schools are human beings, and they don't go away because we fail them—never mind the morality of the issue. Nothing could change schools more, and make them more engaging for students and teachers, than changing our goal to teach individuals versus groups—to say that horrific dropout rates are unacceptable and that we want students to graduate as much as they do—and that we are just as determined as they and their parents are to see that they will succeed and graduate. And that is a huge incentive for students and teachers to persist.

Fully utilize the resources of the portal to individualize instruction digitally and to enhance student engagement. Provide 1:1 technology for every student/teacher, with full digital resources and internet connections. This is blended learning to the max. If we have powerful digital resources for all students and teachers, there is no excuse to keep classrooms and bells—which truly hurt individualization and flexibility and impose major penalties in costs and time for students and for schools. For digital natives, this alone would increase enthusiasm for schooling.

Use software that is different for, or responds to, each individual student's interests and learning styles. Seek out multiple versions of software for different learners pursuing the same studies. Make school choice mean not just choosing a school, but also choosing how to teach and learn, course by course. The Houston ISD has already done this in terms of laptops—but much remains to be done with how the technology is used ("Student 'Compliance Does Not Equal Engagement,'" *Education Week*, Larry Ferlazzo, January 24, 2021, https://www.edweek.org/leadership/opinion-student-compliance-does-not-equal-engagement/2021/01).

Portals are intended to afford students and teachers access to an enormous collection of teaching and learning materials to be used first in schools and on campuses—but which may also be used in other locations including at home. This is not a homeschooling process, but rather an extraordinarily flexible way to teach and learn based on school campuses with teachers—and with the opportunity to use it at home and in other contexts as well.

The lists below identify tools already available online, but teachers, individually and collectively, can create and share teaching materials—and over a very short period the resources will likely grow enormously.

Teachers, students, and parents would find their "favorite sources and approaches" and use them the most. While teachers would not regularly lecture to classes on bell schedules, they could, individually or collectively, elect to do presentations to introduce big ideas, launch courses, etc., and they could elect to create their own digital materials from which students could learn on their own schedules.

Teachers could work individually to prepare complete courses, or they could team up with other teachers to prepare a full set of lectures for a course, and over time this shared collection of lectures would be a wonderful tool by which teachers could plan materials for the needs and interests of each student.

With the focus on outcomes, why not give students and teachers more choices about how they get to the outcomes defined? The following is a list of some tools teachers and students might consider—but this appears to be a tiny subset of the resources available, and schools and teachers will need to collaborate to find the best systems for their needs:

- "The Scramble to Move America's Schools Online," https://www.edweek.org/ew/articles/2020/03/26/the-scramble-to-move-americas-schools-online.html.
- "How Effective Is Online Learning? What the Research Does and Doesn't Tell Us," https://www.edweek.org/ew/articles/2020/03/23/how-effective-is-online-learning-what-the.html.
- "Lessons from a Homeschooling Researcher: What You Should Know Now," https://www.edweek.org/ew/articles/2020/03/27/lessons-from-a-homeschooling-researcher-what-you.html.

- The International Connections Academy Online Private School is a homeschooling resource (https://www.internationalconnectionsacademy.com/about-us) with a different focus than the portal schools proposed here.
- Google Classroom (https://classroom.google.com/h) provides management capabilities and communications for teachers to assure that teachers know what their students are doing.
- Google Slides (https://docs.google.com/presentation/u/0) is a presentation program included as part of the Google Docs office suite offered by Google since 2006.
- PowerPoint is a presentation program released in 1987 that is part of Microsoft Office.
- PowToon (https://www.powtoon.com/blog/best-free-animation-software-for-creating-explainer-videos) is an online presentation software by which to create animated presentations.
- Canva (https://www.canva.com) is a graphic design platform that allows users to create social media graphics, presentations, posters, documents, and other visual content. Users can choose from many professionally designed templates and edit the designs and upload their own photos through a drag-and-drop interface.
- Haiku Deck (https://www.haikudeck.com/education) is used for teaching visual storytelling, presentation techniques, and the creation of memorable lessons.
- Visme (https://www.visme.co) helps teams and individuals scale and control their content creation by centralizing all media assets into one easily accessible location.
- The Intelligent Tutoring System (https://en.wikipedia.org/wiki/Intelligent_tutoring_system) is a Wikipedia piece that lists sixteen sources with extensive education materials.
- Minecraft (https://www.teachingchannel.com/blog/engage-students-minecraft).
- RobotLAB (https://www.robotlab.com).

The coronavirus pandemic forced our schools, businesses, etc., to explore working and communicating via the internet—and that may yet prove to have been a painful way to experience the incredible power and limitations of the internet to connect us for all sorts of purposes—including teaching and learning.

But neither schools nor teachers nor students and their families were sufficiently prepared to use the digital technology. At the same time, all sorts of organizations used software like Zoom to maintain communications, and some of these worked very well and were both convenient and inexpensive for all involved. What are the implications of all that for our schools in the near-term future?

Use the resources of the portal school to afford students, parents, and teachers the opportunity to draw upon the instructional mix of traditional schools, magnet and charter schools, online schools, and homeschooling with continuous service scheduling to create 24/7/365 schooling as appropriate for each student.

Vary instructional methods and software to accommodate each teacher's teaching concepts and styles, and each student's learning styles and paces—multiple teaching and learning approaches for every area of study because one size does not fit all. The school should adapt to its students, not the reverse. Schools and teachers should adapt to students as hospitals and doctors adapt to patients (see *One Size Does Not Fit All: A Student's Assessment of School*, Nikhil Goyal, Alternative Education Resource Organization).

Utilize problem-based/project-based learning to enable each student to become actively engaged in their own learning and to pursue projects that are of particular relevance to them. Doing so inherently individualizes instruction and encourages students to go in different directions while striving for learning objectives. And as students complete their "projects," it allows them to share their work with others and include it in their personal portfolios to show to others in the future.

This has been a huge concept used for decades in schools of architecture (see chapter 4, "Project-Based Learning in an Architectural School") and thoroughly explored in high school teacher Ted McCain's 2021 book *Problems-First Learning* (https://www.solutiontree.com/problems-first-learning.html).

The portal base for faculty and students would be the school's existing classrooms, which would be transformed to provide workstations for the teacher/advisor and students. The teacher/advisor and students would share the space, each with an individual permanent workstation—no one would float. The teacher would advise the students about their overall studies, but may or may not serve as a teacher for any of them. See additional concepts in the "Spaces" section below.

Give students opportunities to make decisions about how, when, and where they work—some responsibility for planning and managing their work, for getting things done, scheduling their time, etc. Students should have a real voice in their studies; everything should not be dictated to them. Having the opportunity to assume more responsibility, to have a real role in managing their studies, would for most students make schooling far more engaging.

That seems to work really well at the Big Picture High Schools, at the Omaha Westside High School, and at the self-directed learning school, Kerr, in the Alief ISD (https://www.aliefisd.net/kerr) (see chapter 5). Also see "Ten

Steps to Better Student Engagement," Tristan de Frondeville, www.edutopia.org/project-learning-teaching-strategies.

Few or no teacher lectures: Reflect on J. Lloyd Trump's 1959 book, *Images of the Future*, and his thoughts about teachers and lectures. Trump contended sixty-two years ago that it is a waste of teachers' time to give the same lecture multiple times each day. He proposed that teachers give the lecture one time/day to a large group of students so that they could spend the rest of the day working with small groups or individuals with more personal interaction.

With today's technology and the portal concept, students could access "lectures" or videos or publications online anytime and anywhere, and teachers and students could interface in diverse ways for the remainder of the day. This is vastly more powerful for learning than lectures.

But preparing lectures is a terrific thought-development process for teachers, and they would still have the opportunity to prepare digital instructional materials for their students—and should share them with other teachers as well. Over time, managing the enormous and constantly changing volume of instructional materials will be a substantial, but wonderful, challenge for teachers, students, schools, and districts.

Assure that every student (and their family) is well known by one or more teachers/advisors at the school. Recall NASSP's *Breaking Ranks: Changing an American Institution* (1996). When a student enrolls in a school, require the parents to make a written contractual commitment to support and participate in their student's schooling. The KIPP schools (see chapter 5) have done this for years with considerable success. This would make schooling more attractive and effective for both students and their parents—and for teachers.

Students and teachers are responsible for realizing learning; they must work together. Recognize learning success for students as the ultimate measure of success for teachers and schools. For school administrators, facilities, staff, and architects, creating a new school building that is in the budget, on time, and does not leak is not sufficient. It must contribute to an atmosphere that breeds success for teachers and students. Look at all the elements of schooling when considering the merits of a school.

Afford students opportunities to work on their own projects—to set their own objectives and schedules—with input and support from their teachers and advisor. Give students exploratory research topics that might lead in multiple directions. Encourage students to team up with other students to undertake substantial projects.

Where appropriate, draw on resources from outside the school to support students on their projects (see chapter 4, "Project-Based Learning in an Architectural School"). Let students find meaning in their work and share it with others. Encourage explorations online and in the community in lieu of, or in addition to, paper or digital "textbook" reading.

Poll students, parents, teachers, and folks in the community, at least once per calendar year, to get their opinions—to see how they think alike and differently—and use the information to shape schooling. Ask all about problems and opportunities in the school related to teaching and learning. Invite students and teachers, individually and collectively, to take a "seat at the table"—to learn about expectations, and to show why and how they can contribute—so they can feel like they are meaningful participants. The digital online learning system should readily facilitate this.

Engage students in assessing their own work. In architectural and project-based learning schools, students participate in group discussions in which they present, discuss, and defend their work with faculty and fellow students. At the Maple Ridge High School, after Ted McCain's students complete their projects, he has them assess their own work and "invoice" him for their grade. It makes students reflect on what they accomplished as backgrounds for their own work in the future. If in assessing their own work, students realize they might have done more in places, Ted allows them to enhance their efforts and resubmit their "invoice."

In lieu of, or in addition to, traditional grades, authentic assessment (which might mean written narratives, portfolios, projects, and exhibitions) could be much more effective for communicating each student's accomplishments ("From Degrading to De-Grading," Alfie Kohn, *High School Magazine*, March 1999, https://www.alfiekohn.org/article/degrading-de-grading).

Students could create and maintain digital portfolios by taking advantage of digital graphic tools to document their own accomplishments as a way to introduce themselves when future opportunities arise. Every student should have the training and software by which to prepare visual materials to support their studies. This is essential in today's visual, graphic world. They can use the portfolios in preparing college applications, and thereafter they can continue to develop and use their portfolios to seek jobs.

This information is a powerful complement to transcripts and grades from teachers and schools. And as students progress and graduate, they could share these portfolios with the school, which could learn from their experiences and accomplishments and therefore help generate the interest and support of both students and parents in the future.

Advisors should track and support the creation and maintenance of students' portfolios. Students (and teachers) should display work they've done via portfolio information they've created in public areas of the school—basically share what they are doing. Students will learn from, stimulate, and encourage each other. This has worked for decades in architecture schools (see chapter 4, "Project-Based Learning in an Architectural School").

Help students envision their own futures. Make it clear that high school is a "stepping stone" to a future yet to be imagined and defined—that it is not the future, not the end itself. Maybe the future is a job, maybe college, etc. Help students consider their future—figure out what they want to do next after high school—and help them explore whatever that is.

Utilize the portal to link each school to its community—and beyond that to the world. Then students and teachers can focus their work on that goal. Take students physically or digitally to see universities, to various businesses, industries, shopping centers, hospitals, factories, art museums, theaters, etc. Have live, constantly changing displays all over the school with information about businesses, news, etc., to stimulate and inform students and teachers.

During the equivalent, in terms of learning realized, of each student's "junior" year, make the creation by the student and their parents, and advisor, of a written plan with aspirations and strategies for the future a prerequisite for the studies yet required for graduation—and an integral part of their digital portfolio.

Promote courses/teaching. Act like students aren't required to take courses—try to stimulate their interests in areas of study through the portal—provide descriptions of why the courses of study might be interesting, helpful, and relevant to their lives. Teachers should prepare materials that promote their subjects in order to help students imagine how the courses would be of interest to their futures.

This info might be provided online, on posters and monitors in school corridors, or in emails to students and their families. "A good course begins with first engaging students with why they might care" (*The Making of a Modern School*, p. 52, Whittle School & Studios, https://www.whittleschool.org/sites/default/files/2019-04/Whittle-Book-2.2.d0cb1064-compressed.pdf).

Do not let a student fail—that is also a school failure. Provide support for individual students and flexible time so that every student succeeds in some manner. Failure is dumb for students (it does not help them learn, costs them time out of their lives, etc.) and for taxpayers (they get to pay again for the same instruction that didn't work in the first place). Nothing is more attractive for a student, or anyone, than pursuing something of value and succeeding.

We need to make it clear to prospective students and parents that they can learn and succeed—regardless of their previous school struggles. KIPP, IDEA, and YES do this well! Question: If a student fails, is it because he/she is dumb or lazy or is it because the school and/or teachers let the student down? The real answer is not as black and white as the question, but things could be very different than they are today.

If we make huge strides toward self-paced instruction with individual supports for students, there may be some that will still fail—but certainly far less. Think about hospitals—if they took the industrial school approach, they would treat all their patients the same, maybe provide some secondary support off to the side in some areas, but write the patient off if that does not work. Hospitals won't do that, so why should our schools? But hospitals still lose some patients.

How to get schools to adopt the attitudes toward failure that characterize hospitals? (See iNACOL's 2010 publication *When Failure Is Not an Option*, https://www.k-12leadership.org/sites/default/files/inacol_failurenotoption.pdf.)

How much are discipline and security problems a function of students who misbehave? Or of the school environment (in which the student does not succeed, is struggling, or thinks that most of school is irrelevant or perhaps is just bored stiff or is treated as a suspect or felon constantly)? How much are things like penitentiary eating environments in school cafeterias generators versus controllers of discipline problems? If students actually wanted to be in a school and to succeed in their studies, would most discipline issues go away?

With individualization, a student won't get kicked out for learning slowly and will get help to try to learn more effectively. What would it do for students' outlooks, perspectives, and attitudes if they knew that the school will not let them fail—that the school will persist with them until they succeed? What if a doctor or hospital said that they would provide treatment for a patient for a fixed period (a semester, for example), and if you aren't cured by that time, they will dump you out the door? Or if you receive a bad lab test report, they will send you back to repeat the exact same treatment that didn't work the first time?

Create art and music programs for twenty-first-century students. Traditional art courses have been largely stuck in the past. Art remains mainly painting, sculpting, and ceramic making—it seems there is minimal to no inclusion for subjects such as digital graphics, photography, video, animation, etc. We should teach these digital arts courses to provide digital literacy skills that students can use in every other course they take—and in the real world to communicate.

Students should keep digital portfolios of their work. There should be digital displays around the campus of student-generated work. Art displays happen in elementary schools and are wonderful—why not in secondary schools? Music should be more than halftime entertainment. John Philip Sousa is OK, but what about Beethoven and Wagner—and even Lady Gaga?

Schools could feature more contemporary music that students love, listen to, write, perform, etc. Why not have live performances every day in some part of the school—in the food court? Why not special programs in the auditorium? Why not "garage bands," or other contemporary formats? Why not a theater that does not entail a giant auditorium? What about black-box productions that are small in scale?

Should programs be the same at all schools or vary from school to school, with students and parents able to choose—or let kids attend one school for their academic studies and go to another for performing arts and/or athletics programs? The arts should be something that more students can enjoy and thereby enjoy their schooling more. The portal concept should apply to every aspect of our schools—not just traditional core academic subjects.

Connect core studies to electives, career programs, and/or projects selected by the students. The objective is to make the core studies more relevant and interesting for the students. There are high schools that have been doing this for years that are very engaging for students:

- The Wunsche Academy High School in the Spring ISD, https://www.springisd.org/wunsche2.
- The Big Picture Schools, https://www.bigpicture.org.
- The Christo Rey school in Minneapolis, https://www.cristoreytc.org.
- The HSPVA and Debakey High Schools in HISD, https://www.houstonisd.org/Domain/22720, https://www.houstonisd.org/debakey.

Reflect on the *instruction methods* used in your school:

- Are the students your school serves as diverse as those in the Houston ISD? Are the outcomes for your students better and more consistent?
- How do the methods of instruction in your school vary from student to student?
- How do teachers and students work together? How do students, teachers, and parents communicate to shape both teaching and learning?

How are students "taught"? What are the responsibilities of the teacher and of the students?

TECHNOLOGY

The objective here is to reflect on how digital technology has and will continue to transform schooling—to recall how digital technology did not replace all that teachers and students needed during the coronavirus pandemic, though it certainly did help. We will consider how technology allows information to come to students and impacts where teaching and learning may occur—and how it can make time much more flexible. How it can give students access to the world anytime and anywhere, how it can change or replace paper libraries, and how it can personalize teaching and learning.

We need to make schools that engage kids who have never known a world without digital technology.

Through the portal and the school's enormous and constantly evolving technology resources, expand teachers', students', and their parents' understanding of how teaching and learning can work, and thereby how it can impact their perspectives on the world around them. This is not a "class" to be taken, but a reality to be experienced. The school will have substantial, robust staff and student development programs to help both learn to use the resources and technology effectively—to realize its potential for teaching and learning.

We must recognize the very long history of our traditional, industrial-age schools and not repeat the mistakes that doomed the open-plan school—which probably would have worked well with different mind-sets about teaching. Thereafter, there will likely need to be frequent updates for everyone as the resources expand and change. One of the school's major responsibilities will be to keep all concerned informed about and comfortable in using the remarkable technology available to them—and everyone involved must recognize that the technology will evolve continuously as the school functions.

Fully individualize teaching and learning digitally. Schooling should be geared to each student's individual background, capabilities, interests, and learning styles. Use far more digital tools and information, and way fewer paper books in every aspect of teaching and learning. Make far more information available to teachers and students in this way—and make it far more accessible and therefore much easier to change constantly to keep it current.

Inform and train both teachers and students about the vast digital resources readily available, thereby giving teachers and students opportunities to explore, create, and communicate in ways easily available to today's students. Consider the vast resources described in *The Google Infused Classroom* (Holly Clark and Tanya Avrith, 2015).

Through the portal school, every student and teacher has a personal digital device with internet access, and they both have access to various output devices—printers, scanners, monitors, 3-D printers, etc. The school, or at least parts, will be open from 8 a.m. to 6 p.m. to give students flexibility with regard to when they can work, and to give students who do not have internet access at home connections through the school itself. At some schools, it may be necessary for parts of the school to be open later into the evenings or even some on weekends. This is explored further in the "Time" section below.

Subjects, content, and instruction can come to students anytime, anywhere, via technology through the portal. Everything students and teachers may need will not be at their campus, but rather can be accessed and acquired via the portal. With technology, dramatic flexibility is available both for what is presented and how it is presented and used. This can change from student to student depending on their progress, learning abilities, and inclinations. If instruction comes to the students, conventional classrooms are not needed and should be converted to house advisories with student and teacher workstations.

Labs, arts, career and technical education (CTE), food services, physical education, etc., will continue to be important. While technology will permit students to continue their studies at home, this is not a homeschooling program—but it will make studying at home and elsewhere possible and more effective when appropriate. See the "Spaces" and "Funding" sections below.

There may be a small paper library as a remnant of the past, but the functional library will be digital and accessible through the portal, and teachers and students will have access to major libraries such as the Library of Congress. The Houston ISD made this change several years ago. Students in other districts in small schools or in rural communities will have exactly the same access to the world's scholarly resources as those in major cities and affluent contexts. Librarians will be research aides and experts in search engines for both faculty and students, and not archivists.

There will be no security devices at library entrances. Libraries will be open, with lots of displays in the area and around the school to attract and inform teachers and students. Reading areas in libraries with tables and chairs will remain to provide places for students to work together when appropriate. Students who do not have internet access at home may use their workstations such as these or other spaces on the campus for studies after normal school hours.

Eliminate 90+ percent of live lectures by delivering instruction to students online, anytime, anywhere—and include all the information formerly delivered via lectures, textbooks, and workbooks, but with vastly more images, videos, sound, links, etc. Recall J. Lloyd Trump's *School for Everyone* (1977, https://www.amazon.com/school-everyone-Design-middle-combines/dp/0882100777).

Even where a live teacher lecture is appropriate, do it most often "live online" (Skype, Zoom, etc.). In lieu of conventional "stand and deliver," teachers could prepare much more sophisticated digital materials and do things they could never do with a marker board—and great presentations could have more impact on far more students. And in lieu of handwritten notes, students could have digital copies of the full lecture, which they could review over and over again as necessary—and add their own highlighting, notes, etc. And if students don't understand everything the first time they see the lecture, allow them to see it repeatedly as needed.

Teachers could prepare online "lectures" or "presentations" and then share them with other teachers in their field across the campus and the district. Teachers could learn from each other and together, creating an enormous and evolving collection of teaching and learning materials to which they could direct individual students based on their learning interests and needs. Teachers could become orchestrators of these teaching and learning resources for the special characteristics of each student.

Imagine that we could realize J. Lloyd Trump's extraordinary educational idea after only forty-four years! How does this relate to the online learning materials students had when working at home during the coronavirus shutdown?

Students who want to take special courses not available on their campus from a teacher there may enroll in the course from a teacher anywhere in the district or possibly from other recognized digital sources anywhere. In this manner, every student and teacher would have access to everything being taught across the entire district and more—the issue of schools in low-income areas or with small enrollments in rural settings having different academic programs from big schools in affluent urban areas would vanish.

But this would put real responsibility on the schools and advisors to inform students about what is available, how to access and use it, etc.

With the technology, the school and its students can draw upon resources from other campuses in the district—from other schools in other cities/states, from publishers of books and professional journals, from faculty in universities, and from businesses in specialized fields such as medicine, banking, chemicals, architecture, engineering, construction, agriculture, transportation, tourism, performing arts, communications/TV, or the internet—just to name a few.

These materials would be available to every student 24/7 wherever they could get online. If students are to write papers, create projects, or take tests along the way, include those in the online materials. A tiny sampling of the vast online resources includes:

- Rice University's OpenStax program, https://openstax.org
- Khan Academy, www.khanacademy.org
- LearnZillion, https://learnzillion.com
- Udacity, www.udacity.com
- Sana Online Learning, https://www.sanalabs.com
- Skillshare, https://skillshare.com
- SparkNotes, https://www.sparknotes.com
- TikTok, https://www.tiktok.com
- Google Teaching Resources, https://edu.google.com/teaching-resources
- We Are Teachers, www.weareteachers.com
- Teachthought, https://www.teachthought.com/technology/100-free-online-resources-for-students

- Intelligent Tutoring Systems (ITS), https://en.wikipedia.org/wiki/Intelligent_tutoring_system
- Open Education Resources: Free Open Education Library, https://www.oercommons.org
- Global Online Academy, https://gobalonlineacademy

Technology enables connection to the world outside schools. Via the portals, technology can link schools to the world around them to make learning much more interesting and relevant for students. Teachers/advisors should make it clear to students that working with stipulated resources is important, but that they are encouraged as well to search for other related sources as they work—and to share those with their fellow students and teachers.

As in airports, office buildings, shopping malls, newsrooms, stock exchanges, restaurants, etc., monitors could provide live information that interests students and faculty. Corridors and commons areas in schools should not be drab, dull, blank spaces with lockers—they should be lively, informative, and help students and teachers develop interests to be explored in their work.

Reflect on the *technology* teachers and students use each day in your school:

- Does every student and teacher have their own digital device and internet access both on campus and at home?
- Are the teaching materials as diverse in their nature as your teachers and students are in their interests and capabilities? Do they evolve as your teachers and students change?
- Does the technology in your school help to optimize teachers' abilities to track their students' progress and to regularly communicate with them?
- Do your students have access to major libraries (such as the Library of Congress, for example)?
- How does the technology in your school facilitate communications between teachers, students, and parents?

TIME

The objective here is to reflect on how school time should change to serve students, and to support and coordinate with other concepts and opportunities. Schools cannot individualize teaching and learning for diverse students with fixed time. Schools cannot realize the potential of digital technology with fixed periods, days, and years. Schools cannot use our teachers and buildings efficiently and effectively with fixed time.

And we cannot respond to huge unknowns like the coronavirus pandemic in ways that serve students, parents, teachers, and communities if the school year is rigidly fixed. Time is very closely linked to all the other elements of schooling. Yet time seems embedded in the back of our skulls, akin to something like gravity, and is rarely discussed—and constrains our thinking and possibilities.

Make school time serve students and learning—time should not drive schooling any more than it should drive hospital processes. Traditional school time is consistently organized with the same amount of time allocated every day for every teacher and subject for every student—regardless of the instruction appropriate for, or the learning realized by, individual students. Time is one of the six elements of schooling; it cannot be set aside in our thinking.

We know with certainty that students (and everyone else) learn in different ways at different paces. But for generations we've said very strongly by our actions that we don't care, that those who don't learn in the time allotted fail, and that those who can finish in less time just have to stick it out. We try with things like AP classes to help students who can move faster, but that does not alter the time frames, only what we try to teach some students. If we could make time flexible, it would make schooling much more personalized, which would remove huge pressures for succeeding.

In response to this flexible time structure, parents will probably be very encouraging about their children getting after their studies and graduating. Some parents might chafe a bit if their thirty-five-year-old is still in high school and living at home. The flexibility and parental expectations make a strong combination with each student's aspirations (*Prisoners of Time*, April 1994, https://files.eric.ed.gov/fulltext/ED489343.pdf; "Want to Improve Learning Outcomes? Give Students More Time," Pam Grossman, *Education Week*, https://www.edweek.org/leadership/opinion-want-to-improve-learning-outcomes-give-students-more-time/2021/03).

Students advance when they achieve mastery in competency-based learning, not merely a C or D, which leaves them ill prepared for other studies to follow in secondary and postsecondary schooling—and in the world after school. While many students may continue to complete their studies in the traditional four years, others may graduate in less than, or more than, four years depending on their capabilities and the pace of their studies (see *When Failure Is Not an Option: Designing Competency-Based Pathways for Next Generation Learning*, iNACOL, https://files.eric.ed.gov/fulltext/ED514435.pdf, and *Breaking with Tradition: The Shift to Competency-Based Learning in PLCs at Work*, Brian Stack and Jonathan Vander Els, 2017, https://www.solutiontree.com/breaking-with-tradition.html).

Transcripts and school records should note when students reached mastery learning. They should not indicate when students began their studies and if they withdrew from a course without achieving mastery learning, there should be no record of their efforts.

Set graduation as the goal for every student—no dropping out. States across the U.S. have set varied compulsory education requirements, including when children must start school and when they can drop out legally ("State Laws on Ages When Children Must Attend School," https://www.lawyers.com/legal-info/research/education-law/chart-age-requirements-for-compulsory-education-in-all-50-states.html). But these focus on "ages," not "learning." We should not set an age (such as those ranging from sixteen to nineteen years in various states per the list noted above) when students may simply drop out. Why do we have capability standards for driver's licenses and all sorts of jobs, but not minimal education standards for being a citizen and voter? That makes sense only with today's rigid school years and mass instruction.

We should make special provisions to optimize school for students with limited capabilities and/or special needs, but otherwise, every student should be strongly supported in completing their required studies. How differently would students and parents approach K–12 education if students cannot simply wait out their time and drop out? We should help students succeed—not abandon them. We should help them envision and realize success for their own futures.

Make schooling a continuous service that is provided all year, like medical services and hospitals. The agrarian calendar makes no sense today for our students, families, teachers, schools, communities, or economy. If schooling was a continuous service, the terrible interruptions to both K–12 and postsecondary schools caused by the coronavirus in 2020–2021 would have been less severe—still difficult, but easier for students and teachers to accommodate. Teachers and students may attend all year or part of the year at paces that work for their learning and families.

This would improve learning and utilize both staff and facilities much more efficiently (see "Spaces" and "Funding" sections below), but we would have to set some minimum levels of study for students to qualify as a "student" and avoid truancy laws. Schooling would still be required—only parents and students would now have flexibility about how to meet the objectives. The rate of schooling should be defined over a calendar year so that students and parents could elect to have time off during any season of the year—not just during the summer months. Making time more flexible would make schooling both more effective and more attractive.

Schooling as a continuous service would be considerably less costly if schools could use facilities all year—serving more students in the same facilities. Teachers could elect to teach some or all of the school year and make varied salaries. Those teaching full time would make more than today's teachers do for a nine-month school year.

There should be no bells that pace/limit teaching and learning time. There should be no "learn on schedule or fail and repeat." Absent bells and passing periods, every secondary school student and teacher will gain approximately a half hour of time each day for more productive efforts than jostling their way through crowded corridors.

With limited, fixed time per period or class, the opportunity for teachers and individual students to get to know each other is very limited. If most content delivery is digital, enabling students and teachers to connect on an "as needed" basis, teacher-student relationships would change profoundly—and student-to-student contact could evolve as well.

Absent classes and bells, the need to eliminate penalties for students being late to class or skipping classes emerges. If schools don't have bells, classes, and group lectures—how can a school tell if a student is late to class? It is much more effective for teachers and advisors to solely track how students are progressing in their studies via the software they use—the work that they are actually doing.

But we must be clear about students' commitments to meet with advisors and teachers in special subjects with special facilities (CTE, science, visual/performing arts, etc.). And, through the advisors and parents, schools must clearly set high expectations for the ideal level of work students must do in order to reach the required learning objectives.

The real measure of a student's work will be known from monitoring online studies and observing the work completed. Advisors should review this work with students and parents as appropriate to help the learning advance. In general, the school, advisors, and parents should make students' management of their own time every student's responsibility and support them in the effort. This sort of skill is important for everyone. If they don't fulfill time commitments for realizing goals, their time-management problems will show up in all sorts of important places outside school later in life.

With flexible scheduling, separate participation in seasonal extracurricular programs (athletics) from schooling. If students want to participate in extracurricular programs, they must sustain some defined level of studies during the season of their activity to be eligible. Flexible student schedules should not be used to permit "full-time" athletes and competitive advantages relative to other schools with conventional schedules.

Provide athletic programs at some portal schools, but not all—like magnet and choice schools do currently. Schedule athletics and related performing arts programs that involve large groups of students late in the day to minimize conflicts with scholastic studies.

Help students succeed; never label students failures based on the pace of their learning—maybe there are "slow succeeders," but there are no failures. If a student completes all the learning required for a course in six weeks, congratulate him/her and get them started on the next area of study; remember Mozart and Mendelsohn—and J. Lloyd Trump's *School for Everyone*. If another student in the same course needs fifteen weeks to complete the learning required, give him/her a pat on the back and get them to work on their next area of study.

Be mindful of the "custodial" role of schools. If we make time, not learning, flexible, we need to be mindful of the "custodial" role schools play in "caring" for students—even high school students during the school day. And we should redefine the "school day." Maybe it means that students will need to define what they are going to do each day, how long they will be in the school, and attend on a schedule that works for, and is approved by, their parents and advisor (the school).

One giant advantage of advisories is that students have individual workstations and can work there to take advantage of the time they have on campus. If students and teachers have workstations in the school, they should have access to them for something like a conventional "workday"—from 8 a.m. to 5 or 6 p.m. They do not have to be sitting in a "class" under the gaze of a teacher. They will have a degree of "supervision" from their advisor and the overall school.

If they want to stay and "hang out" on the campus and work, be around their friends, have access to teachers, etc., that would be super for students and parents—and probably for their learning as well. This works very well in architectural schools (see chapter 4) where students use their architectural studio spaces for all their courses/studies—not just architecture.

If we could individualize much more with advisories, technology, and self-pacing, we would have a much better opportunity to address the needs of diverse students—as the KIPP schools do (https://www.kipp.org/school/kipp-houston-high-school). Ideally, there would be a mix of ages of students in each advisory that reflects the mix in the school so that the school does not have "levels" of advisories. Could the advisors do things differently with both students and parents on an individual basis? Could the advisors be complemented by counselors or others in addressing the needs of individual students?

Wouldn't this work if all the students in each advisory are self-paced—doing different things each day? Wouldn't a mix of students of different ages in each advisory be beneficial as older students nearing graduation mentor younger students just beginning? Wouldn't a mix of students of diverse ethnicities and economic backgrounds give each student a broader perspective about the world and their own aspirations, opportunities, and possibilities?

Reflect on the *time* teachers and students have each day and each year in your school:

- Are the days in your school divided into periods between which students move from teacher to teacher and classroom to classroom? Are the lengths of grading periods, semesters, and school years fixed for students and teachers?
- How does the organization of time in your school support teaching and learning? How does it accommodate students with diverse learning abilities and paces?
- If a student in your school realizes the learning objectives of a course more quickly than the defined time schedule or, conversely, learns more slowly and needs more time, how does your school treat these variations?
- Reflect on the cost to build and to operate your school building and its site. Is your school using these substantial capital improvements efficiently over the full calendar year?

SPACES

The objective here is to describe and explore the spaces that will be required to support schooling that is more attractive for students and teachers—the sorts of workspaces each will need, how the character of those spaces can contribute to the engagement of students, how those spaces can be organized so that moving within them is an enriching experience, and how we can use those spaces more efficiently and effectively. The intent is to explain why the "classroom" is not the only place, or even the best place, where teaching and learning can occur.

We can preserve the school facilities we have and the immense investments they represent by repurposing classroom spaces to house teacher/advisor and student workstations. These individual assigned workstations for both teachers and students will be permanent bases for them with provided power, internet access, and secured storage for their working materials and personal items. We can also retain other facilities and site improvements for administration, science labs, CTE, visual/performing arts, PE/athletics, etc., and preserve the library's reading areas and the librarian's office and conference spaces but delete or modify stack spaces to house teacher/advisor workstations like those located in the school's former classrooms.

Organize schools around groups of advisories (each a former classroom with workstations for a teacher/advisor and a group of students), not around classes or disciplines. In each group of advisories, be sure that teachers are from different core disciplines, to be readily accessible to the students in the advisory. They may not actually "teach" any of the students in their advisory but would be available as resources when needed by individual students. Define groups of related advisories with graphics (room names/numbers with that of their teacher/advisor), not by modifying partitions or spaces.

Group student workstations around that of an advisor who serves the group as a counselor, guide, friend, mentor, and monitor—who knows each student and his/her parents well and works with them throughout their years at the school—and who is a teacher in their area of expertise and works with students primarily online, but also in person when appropriate.

Each advisory houses students from each grade level, and they remain together with their advisor as some start and others graduate for their full time at the school. The continuity with the advisor and other students assures each student a "base" in the school in which they know all those in their immediate surroundings.

Every student has a digital link to their teacher in every class, but for additional support, they may visit with teachers in their own advisory/small learning community as well. Interspersed with the flexible student and teacher workstations, there would be small conference areas to accommodate group discussions. Quite intentionally, this is highly flexible and would evolve as students work, progress, and succeed. It is much more supportive and individualized than traditional schooling organized around disciplines, classrooms, and bells.

Optimize the enrollment capacity of school facilities. The capacity of traditional school facilities to serve students is not the total number of seats in teaching spaces but is a function of how those spaces are utilized over time. Traditional classrooms are used for instruction with students about 75 percent of the typical school day and are used as teachers' offices the remaining 25 percent of each day.

And, with the agrarian calendar, most classrooms serve students about 75 percent of each school day and 75 percent of the calendar year (nine school months out of the twelve-month year), or about 56 percent of the year. If teaching and learning could occur throughout the calendar year, we would substantially increase the enrollment capacities of our existing school facilities and thereby reduce facility costs per student.

If additional capacity is required or special links to the community, create advisory groups/small learning communities in non-school buildings near the school—in leased office or retail structures, for example. Schools could be created that are part of, not separate from, the communities they serve. Link these communities to the main campus via the same technology used by all students and teachers. This could give schools a high degree of flexibility to serve different enrollments as communities change over time, and to respond to varying circumstances as to where school facilities might be most accessible and effective.

Provide specialized spaces and equipment for core subjects (such as science) in every small learning community or nearby, or use digital labs and spaces where possible. Most likely students could use these on their own schedules as required by their individual progress in their studies. Such labs could be staffed by assistant teachers. Westside High School in Omaha (https://westside66.org) has been doing this since the 1960s.

Encourage students to "personalize" their workstations just as teachers do in current classrooms or as employees in offices do. Students may not need lockers if they may store their personal effects at their workstations. Such workstations give students a real sense of belonging in the school and afford them a much better opportunity to get to know, and to be known by, adults such as their advisor.

The School of Environmental Sciences (aka the Zoo School, https://sesmn.org) in Minneapolis has had these since it was founded in 1996. Each student remains in their advisory for the duration of their years in the school. Over time, some students will complete their studies and graduate, and others will join the advisory and begin their studies. Advisories provide continuous, supportive environments for teachers and students.

Make school corridors as interesting as urban sidewalks or shopping malls. What would happen if we thought of students as "customers" to be attracted versus "attendees" mandated to be there by truancy laws and who must be controlled? What if we recognized charters and private schools as competitors? We could make schools much more interesting spatially by lining them with things such as displays or monitors that interest students. It seems amazing that corridors in elementary schools are almost always encrusted with wonderful student artwork, but secondary schools are not.

We should get rid of or cover up lockers and instead use those corridors to show off what is happening in the school and the outside world by displaying student work via big video monitors. If all students kept digital portfolios related to their studies, that could be displayed on walls just like in art and architecture schools. They should also include presentations that teachers have prepared with the intent of attracting students to courses. Displays could also be prepared by companies, professions, and universities—not advertisements, but rather info about the real world and future career possibilities that is interesting for both students and teachers and that will lead them to seek out more information, discuss it with peers/colleagues, etc.

Who might make these sorts of "displays" in/for schools? There are companies, such as Conference Technologies, that could help districts make schools lively, fascinating places (https://www.conferencetech.com/aboutus). Some other potential sources include:

- Outside sources: instructional material producers—folks who create digital instructional materials accessible via the portal. Could they make displays by simply extracting things from their digital materials and present it on monitors or projection walls or posters? See the list in chapter 3.
- What about trade organizations or major corporations? Would they provide digital materials about real-world products and services that could excite students through exposure?
- Could displays be extracted from advertisements? From the firms that make ads?
- Could displays be obtained from major professional organizations about the nature of their field—teachers, doctors, lawyers, architects, engineers, developers, contractors, actors, musicians, chefs, manufacturers, pilots, etc.?
- What about local visual and performing arts groups such as art museums, theaters, symphonies, operas, and rock groups?
- Could we have displays from universities/colleges about what they offer to help students aspire to things they might never have seen or imagined? Universities, not to mention businesses, advertise and recruit "customers"—it should not be hard to get information from them.
- What about things related to travel: airlines, resorts, hotels, countries, and cities that attract tourists by the millions. What about guidebook publishers like Michelin, EyeWitness, Lonely Planet, Bradt, Rough Guides, Insight Guides, Time Out, Footprint, Blue Guides, Marco Polo, and Cicerone?
- What about parents and families? Could we get them to do displays related to their work? Could we get families to share images related to their travels? Could we get them to help inform and excite students?
- Could teachers generate displays about what they teach, both required and elective subjects? Displays with a real focus on stuff students need to learn? If teachers don't have to "stand and deliver," would they now have time for making displays to attract students? Could students help teachers make those displays, and thereby learn about the subject matter at the same time?
- Could schools have major displays related to projects by students? Could the culmination of each project be a "display" to show other students about the interesting things they've done? Could the school make videos of student presentations and show them? Could materials students prepare for their portfolios be used to let everyone see the

work being done? Architecture schools have always done this—and the students excite each other.
- Could the context of the school be part of the excitement? So often we isolate schools from everything else—see the huge sites ringed by chain-link fences in the suburbs. We argue that the isolation is good for security or that the schools are near where students live. Could schools happen in the midst of busy commercial areas where real life is happening (see *Palaces for the People*, Eric Klinenberg, https://www.amazon.com/Palaces-People-Infrastructure-Inequality-Polarization/dp/1524761168)?
- Could we use displays to help expose students (particularly low-socioeconomic students who may have limited exposure opportunities) to interesting things they may not have seen or experienced?

How to overcome the idea that all this will distract students? Absent traditional lectures with students lined up in rows, would distractions be an issue? Students already sit on the floor in Barnes & Noble stores with a cup of Starbucks and their laptops and read and study. People (including students) read and work in restaurants, on trains, at airports, and on airplanes. How can we make schools where students want to come just as much as they want to go to Starbucks? How can we go to sidewalk cafés and restaurants and yell at each other over the din, and yet still have memorable, enjoyable conversations when schools have to be quiet and focused?

Could it be that the way we are teaching does not turn kids on and attract or merit their undivided attention? How is it that people can work in offices that have no partitions—just open workstations—and do complex work with people walking around talking on phones, working on keyboards, etc.—but that can't work in schools? And a bunch of those folks these days have earbuds linked to some digital source.

Maybe this is a generational issue (digital immigrants vs. natives), but maybe it is an exposure issue with educators versus people who work in other fields/environments. Other fields work in these spaces because of the flexibility, because of the communication, and because of the collaboration needed. Schools act like they don't need the flexibility, don't want communication except for teachers to students, and don't think they need the collaboration.

Creating advisories by refurnishing former classrooms should preserve their quiet working atmospheres, but absent class periods, bells, and passing periods, the corridors and public spaces that link them together should be much livelier and more interesting every day for students and faculty.

There are enclosed, secured specialized spaces for some science labs, CTE programs, performing/visual arts, and PE/athletics. Ideally, these specialized spaces are dispersed about the school to make them an integral part of the environment, and wherever possible have some openings or transparent walls and special displays to inform students and faculty about what happens within them. Access to advisories with teacher/advisor and student workstations should probably be controlled (card keys, for example) during certain hours of the day/week.

While digital teaching and learning materials and time are the major factors in making the school flexible and responsive to change in the future, furnishings in advisories for teachers and students should be created from highly flexible furniture systems extensively used for decades in corporate office settings. These systems would allow teachers/advisors, students, and maintenance staff to make substantial changes whenever helpful, with little to no need for construction staff and the subsequent related time and costs.

Some example sources:

- Urban Office, https://www.urban-office.com/index.html.
- Herman Miller, https://www.hermanmiller.com.
- Steelcase, https://www.steelcase.com.
- Humanscale, https://ca.humanscale.com/index.cfm.
- Knoll, https://www.knoll.com/design-plan.

If the existing school from which the portal school is to be created has natural light in classrooms, that should be carefully preserved. The natural light is beneficial for students and faculty. In the past, some educators have argued that natural light and views to the exterior are distractions for students, but if we make school spaces more humane, would we find that students are better behaved and more engaged? Why would we strive to provide natural light in office buildings but not in schools? Do windows distract office workers and reduce their efficiency, productivity, and the money they earn? In traditional schools, is natural light the distraction, or is the distraction the way instruction works?

School safety and security relate equally to students and teachers/advisors. There is a dreadful and long history of school violence (see the Wikipedia list: https://en.wikipedia.org/wiki/List_of_attacks_related_to_secondary_schools). We now have schools with entry vestibules to screen visitors and limit access, and even some with metal detectors and X-ray units exactly like those in airports.

Many schools have, for a long time, been substantially isolated from the communities they serve by virtue of their location in residential areas, and big sites with playfields and perimeter chain-link fences. Wikipedia's history clearly shows that the majority of school security incidents have involved students who were enrolled in the schools. Provisions to secure our schools have not made schooling more attractive to students or teachers. If we could change the atmosphere in schools by truly personalizing teaching and learning to help students succeed in their learning, could we also make schools safer?

Make food services available throughout the school day. Food services should follow the same flexible scheduling provided for teaching and learning. Do not have eating spaces with long rows of penitentiary tables and fixed seating. This is done for control and janitor convenience, but it's terrible for people—and students are people! Try to imagine a restaurant where people choose the same environments we have provided in school cafeterias for decades. Do schools have food fights because they are so much more fun than what is allowed?

If learning was individualized and self-paced, if there were no bells, if students and teachers could eat when they are hungry, and if the food service could be spread out over much more of the school day, could we make eating in schools a pleasure and provide smaller cafeterias—and therefore save considerable square footage and costs?

Or could we avoid big cafeterias altogether and disperse small serveries among the advisories so that students and teachers could eat in their advisories at or near their workstations? Office workers do this every day. Would students or teachers make a mess while eating at their own desks which they must use throughout the day? The Christo Rey school in Minneapolis has done this for years. The updated Lamar High School in Houston that opened in the fall of 2019 has learning communities each with its own food service.

While the food service should provide meals over defined periods, snacks and beverages should be available throughout the day. The school should leave the existing cafeteria/dining space(s) open throughout the school day but with flexible furnishings so that students and teachers may also use the spaces for meetings, discussions, eating snacks, etc. In between meals, the serveries should function like Starbucks to give students and teachers places to meet that also have access to beverages and snacks.

Could school dining spaces be more like food courts in shopping malls? Students seem to behave and enjoy themselves in these environments. Why not in schools? Additionally, high schools could allow upperclassmen to eat off campus. The Westside High School in Omaha has been doing this for decades, provided that students maintain their studies. Regardless, if students are on flexible schedules, some will need to come and go during the day—and eating can be part of that process (see flexible time notes above).

Reflect on the *spaces* that house and serve your teachers and students every day:

- Does every teacher and every student have a place of their own in which to work—or do some of them float?

- Are the spaces arranged to support ideal relationships between teachers and students?
- Are the spaces in your school "alive" with information related to what is being taught in the school? Is your school a lively, interesting place in which to work?
- Are the spaces, furnishings, and supporting technology networks sufficiently flexible to accommodate the changes inherent in the world outside our schools?
- Is your school's cafeteria an attractive, enjoyable space that is open and lively all day?

COMMUNITY

The objective here is to explore how instructional programs, facilities, and schedules should relate to the community the school serves, how parity should first be measured in terms of outcomes for students rather than money per student, and how schools should relate to their communities in terms of their programs, spaces, activities, and use of time. Also examined are how schools might be part of, instead of isolated from, the communities they serve and how things in the community could enhance the schooling, student interest, engagement, and sense of relevance.

Change the meaning of "attendance zones"—create diverse schooling (see February 2015 article, "How a Portfolio of Schools Meets Students' Needs," https://www.ascd.org/el/articles/how-a-portfolio-of-schools-meets-students-needs). Attendance zones were good for Taylor/Wirt efficient use of school services and spaces, but when they mean comparable/standardized teaching and learning processes, materials, technology, time, facilities, and funding for different students, they virtually preclude comparable learning outcomes for diverse individual students.

We should convert attendance zones into strategies for distributing students among "portals" to utilize their capacities for student and teacher advisories most efficiently, from which they would access the teaching and learning services of the entire district and not just what is physically available on that campus. Additionally, there should be flexibility for students and their parents with regard to attending other schools to access other special programs.

"Attendance zones" should be preserved only as a way to distribute students and faculty to various facilities/campuses as their "bases" from which to access the system and use existing facilities effectively. But instructional resources, practices, etc., will draw via the portal system from the full district, not just the campus or attendance zone—and this access will be the same for every student at every school (see figure 2.3).

Students (and their diplomas) will be identified by the district first and by the campus(es) where they are based second, if at all. Every campus must seek to identify itself in ways that will attract both students and faculty. If one school is packed and another half empty, the schools (and district) need to rethink programs and how the schools attract students.

Transforming existing traditional schools to portal schools could truly provide comparable access for every student to all of the same teaching and learning resources, and greatly increase each student's opportunities for success. Schools would still vary in terms of their staff and the contexts in which they are located and from which they could draw, but with each district and each school's digital links, the opportunities to share vast bodies of teaching and learning materials and processes would transform schooling.

Provide magnet schools, CTE programs, and spaces in schools where they can attract diverse enrollments—and ideally from which they can draw resources—like the Debakey High School for Health Professionals near the Houston Medical Center, or the Kinder High School for the Performing Visual Arts near the performing arts venues in downtown Houston, or schools focused on various industries along the ship channel, or a school focused on real estate/development near downtown or the Galleria, or a school focused on aviation like the Christo Rey school near Hobby Airport. Our giant cities provide a rich context from which we should draw for CTE programs that get students informed and excited about various fields of study/work.

If within the portal school structure districts wish to preserve traditional public school types (charter, magnet, online schools, and homeschooling), parents and students must still select their school. However, the process of selecting schools would be simplified because, with the portal system, every campus truly has access to comparable digital instructional materials and the related individualized processes.

Schools must still create programs, facilities, and staff that satisfy the objectives of the parents and students and are also competitive with those of other schools. As various forms of school choice grow, the process becomes more critical to both schools and parents/students.

Bernie Bleske's article, "School and the Tomato: Education Is No Longer a Monopoly" (https://medium.com/age-of-awareness/school-and-the-tomato-2e79605de6ac), provides some interesting perspectives on schools and choice. This means that individual schools would not be guaranteed students by attendance zones anymore. With school choice and diverse schools, each would have to attract students to use their capacities and faculty. The giant "trick" here will be to figure out how to help parents and students do this well and take it seriously. For the sake of the student and parents, and the schools, this process should be realized for each student early in the equivalent of their last year of junior high school.

50   Chapter 2

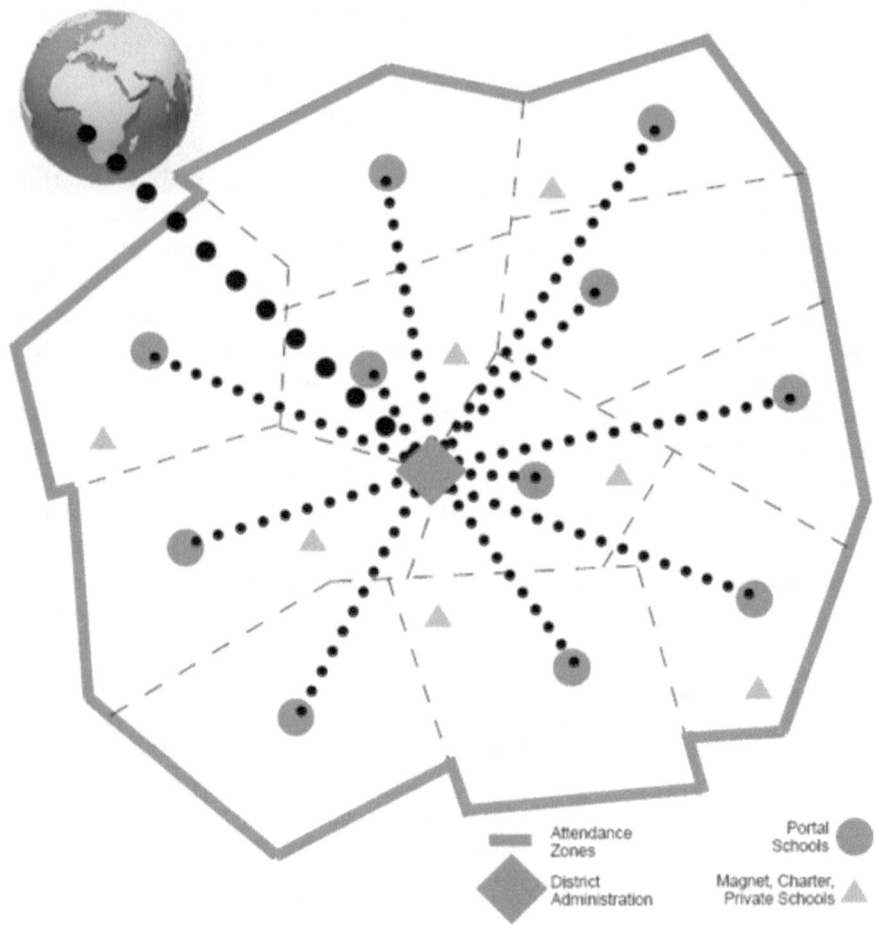

PORTAL SCHOOLS DISTRICT STRUCTURE

Attendance zones remain only as guides for the District, students and parents. Admission to individual schools is based on applications with priorities given to residents within the attendance zones. Through the District, every school, teacher and student have direct online access 24/7 to every course in every school, and all have access to the Library of Congress and worldwide resources. Teacher/Advisors work closely with students to help them utilize the system, stimulate their interests, and realize meaningful learning. The school facilities operate 5 days/week (8-6) and are accessible on Saturdays. Students and teachers may work on different schedules. Students must realize mastery learning in every subject, may graduate in more/less than 4 years. Schools offer diverse CTE, performing/visual arts and athletic programs. Students document their studies with digital portfolios. Schools are alive with constantly changing displays about the world they serve and help students to explore their own futures.

Figure 2.3. Diagram of a school district: Portal schools district structure. *Author created.*

Build and promote the identity/reputation of each school first around its academics—not its mascots and extracurricular activities. Many schools, even elementary schools, are better known for their fierce mascots and/or their sports teams rather than their teaching and learning. Could we make schools where students and parents are proud of their academics—and have mascots that won't eat students?

In that regard, consider Rice University's "owl" in comparison to other schools' panthers or rattlesnakes or pirates—what do these choices say to students and the public? Consider Harvard, a truly exceptional and very well-known university. What is its mascot? Maybe "mascots" are a distraction as a part of a school's identity?

Academic achievements are almost invisible. Could we reverse that by touting what the school's students have done, such as academic prizes they've won, super test scores they've earned, etc.? What about touting where the school's graduates have gone to college and what they've done after school or college, e.g., highlighting successful and/or famous alumni? Why not make this part of the displays around the school that were discussed earlier in this chapter? For example, the KIPP High School in Houston displays banners from the universities in which their graduates have enrolled.

Why not have academic school spirit in lieu of, or in addition to, sports spirit only? Why not have display cases full of current/evolving academic trophies and not just old athletic trophies? If football coaches can find their jobs in jeopardy after several losing seasons, shouldn't principals and teachers have the same problem with low student performance?

Schools should set high academic standards and promote their academic accomplishments. That should attract more students and their parents than a winning sports team—particularly if more folks grasped the value of learning, and there are schools that have way more applicants than seats every year and have no sports programs or snarling mascots. How can we stir up that sort of interest for more and more schools?

- DeBakey High School for Health Professions, https://www.houstonisd.org/debakey.
- Kinder High School for the Performing and Visual Arts, https://www.houstonisd.org/Domain/22720.
- Wunsche High School, https://www.springisd.org/wunsche2.
- New Tech High @ Coppell, https://www.coppellisd.com/site/default.aspx?domainid=1912.

Searching for Schools

Parents and students must obtain detailed information by which to facilitate their exploration of potential schools. Listed below are examples from sources in Texas, but it seems quite probable that there are comparable sources in other cities, school districts, and states. Clearly, all these sources would complement visits to individual campuses and discussions with their staff.

- The Texas Education Agency, Texas Academic Performance Reports (https://tea.texas.gov/perfreport/tapr/index.html), provides detailed information on every public school in Texas.
- C@R (Children at Risk) Texas School Rankings (https://texasschoolguide.org/school-rankings) also provides detailed information on every public school in Texas and ranks how they've performed.
- GreatSchools Rating, https://www.greatschools.org/gk/ratings.
- School Solutions (Carolyn Means, cfmeans44@gmail.com) is an independent educational consultant who works with families to search for and select schools. If parents and students had more choices, it seems virtually certain there would be many more such consultants, including some from the school districts themselves.

Assessing Schools

Schools and districts should maintain consistent, readily accessible statistics about all of their schools so that parents and students may see how individual campuses are performing. That information is accessible today in Houston and Texas (see data sources above), but students and parents need real guidance in finding and using these sources. The most important part of schools competing with each other should be the learning outcomes realized by their students—and the public needs to know how to find that information.

School Locations

Some schools, in particular elementary schools, are located in residential neighborhoods, while others are located in more lively, active parts of the community that also contain retailers, offices, businesses, etc., where students are exposed to, and may learn from, the world for which their schooling is preparing them. The locations of schools should be carefully planned as our communities grow and evolve, but in many cities like Houston, there is little to no coordination between urban planning and school planning. That is unfortunate for students and schools as well as for our urban environments. School districts and city governments should coordinate their efforts to locate and develop school sites.

Some schools are physically separated from their surrounding contexts by large sites, playfields, and fences. In theory, this helps make the schools safe and secure, but it may do just the opposite. Such separations diminish schools' and students' opportunities to participate in and contribute to the community environment. Could schools be more secure and contribute more to their communities by being more closely linked to their surroundings?

How does this relate to the "social infrastructure" Eric Klinenberg described in *Palaces for the People*?

Reflect on the *community* surrounding your school and the broader city of which your school is a part:

- How diverse are the families and students in your community? Are some of your students consistently realizing better outcomes than others?
- What percentage of your students graduate in four years and continue with postsecondary studies?
- What are you doing to help all of your students realize good outcomes?
- How do the programs within your school draw from resources in the community that it serves? Do the programs afford students unique learning opportunities? Do some of the resources provide support for school programs that benefit teaching and learning?
- How does your campus/school building relate to the community of which it is a part? Is it a lively part of the community used by lots of folks, or is it carefully secured to protect the school, students, and teachers?
- Is your school a real asset to its community? Does the school contribute to the community by attracting new residents?

FUNDING

The objective here is to explore how school funds could be used more effectively to realize our teaching and learning aspirations and to explore how we could use teachers, facilities, and technology more efficiently, which would result in increasing their capacities and reducing their cost per graduate.

Facilities and Staff Costs

Schools would provide continuous education services all year, just like hospitals and most businesses. Teachers and students, like doctors and patients, would have flexibility within that context about when they contribute to/participate in those services. But, relative to traditional schools and agrarian calendars, the utilization of facilities could be substantially increased, which will provide more facility capacity for costs comparable to those incurred today. Teachers may elect to teach more or less than they do today, and their compensation could vary accordingly.

Time Costs

The traditional rigid school year has huge cost ramifications in terms of facilities and teachers. It makes no sense at all to use school facilities only 75 percent of the calendar year when most facility costs continue while schools are closed during the summer months. And it gets worse when one considers that classrooms are rarely used for instruction or to serve students more than 75 percent of the time during the school year—so 75 percent of 75 percent = 56.25 percent of the calendar year. Do taxpayers understand the funding implications of the typical school calendar and teaching procedures?

School Costs

The costs of schooling should be computed as the cost per graduate, not the cost per seat warmed. Traditionally, we compute the cost per student per year regardless of whether the schooling was effective and learning objectives were realized or not.

The cost per graduate measures all the school's costs against the number of students who were successful in their learning—and this cost per graduate would very clearly identify those schools where teaching and learning are not working well because the cost per graduate would be very much higher than the cost per seat warmed. The lowest-performing schools would be considerably more costly than the highest-performing schools—and the public would properly be concerned about that.

Technology Costs

Some students have more technology at home than in their schools. If 1:1 technology and internet connections are available to every student 24/7, would we get more teaching and learning done each day without the limitations of traditional school hours? Could the capacity of schools grow if instruction is not totally linked to seat counts? Could we much more easily and economically realize individualized instruction and thereby get better results for each student? Could having digital access to instructional materials and faculty make just about everything available to every student regardless of the size and location of the school?

Did we learn anything about the role of technology from shutting down schools and/or "homeschooling" as part of the COVID-19 process? Could we spend less on facilities by using them more efficiently and therefore have more to spend on technology?

Reflect on the *funding* required to sustain your school and its staff, students, and programs:

- How do you measure the cost of operating your school, and how does that "measure" reflect the success of your programs and students? Do you compute the cost per student served in the school or the cost per successful teaching and learning, i.e., the cost per graduate?
- Do you operate your site, facilities, technology, and staff continuously throughout the calendar year, or is the school substantially shut down for some significant time periods?
- Do you tout the success of your students in terms of their postsecondary studies and successes? Do you display materials from previous graduates' portfolios in the school as a stimulus for your current students and as a way to attract more students in the future?

PORTAL SCHOOLS

Reflect on the portal schools concepts and consider Michael McQueen's June 2020 blog post "Why We Should Rethink the 3 R's of Education" (https://michaelmcqueen.net/blog/why-we-should-rethink-the-3-r-s-of-education). Below are excerpts from his blog post:

- "The fundamental place for future preparation, you would expect the schooling system to be ahead of its time with its eyes on the future, but as the world had changed rapidly in recent decades, it has proved itself prone to walking in the steps of the past."
- "Central to the changes necessary will be a shift in paradigm from delivering content to students to building capabilities within them."
- "The goal needs to move from the approach of 'students learning from the teacher in lecture mode' to students 'teaching themselves with the teacher's guidance.'"
- "When the future of work centers around collaboration, flexibility, and originality, an education system based on silent work, predictability, and rote-learning is problematic."

So the question is, will we change our schools?

NOTE

1. "Across Texas, More and More English Learner Students Find the Language Barrier Harder to Overcome," April 14, 2021, Kinder Research Institute, https://kinder.rice.edu/urbanedge/2021/04/14/texas-public-schools-more-english-learners-take-longer-proficiency?mc_cid=fc6d10cbe8&mc_eid=1b2d868587.

Chapter 3

Creating Portal Schools

It is one thing to have a "good idea" for improving your school, but it's quite another to deal with all the elements of schooling and realize the good idea. The objective here is to describe the transformation of existing secondary schools to function as portal schools by preserving our enormous investment in school facilities and by engaging teachers, parents, and students in the process of making schooling for the future. The intent here is to very briefly outline the planning, funding, design, construction, and staff development processes so that readers from all sorts of different backgrounds can clearly see how everything might fit together.

Among the struggles in the past with transforming schools to realize new concepts for teaching and learning are the enormous costs and time involved, and the disruptions for teachers, students, and communities. The intent of portal schools is that they can be created within existing school facilities with relatively minor changes and with the teaching and technology changes we've already seriously explored and begun, even before the COVID-19 pandemic.

The diagram in figure 3.1 describes the transformation process, organized in five phases, for a substantial high school in a major urban context. It shows how the transformation could be realized over two years while the school continues in operation. Calendar years are indicated across the top of the diagram, while traditional school years are defined by the gray tones in the background.

COMMUNITY TO BE SERVED: EXISTING PROGRAMS AND FACILITIES

The process must begin with an analysis of the broad community (not just the school's attendance zone), the nature and number of the students currently being served, and how that enrollment might evolve in the foreseeable future.

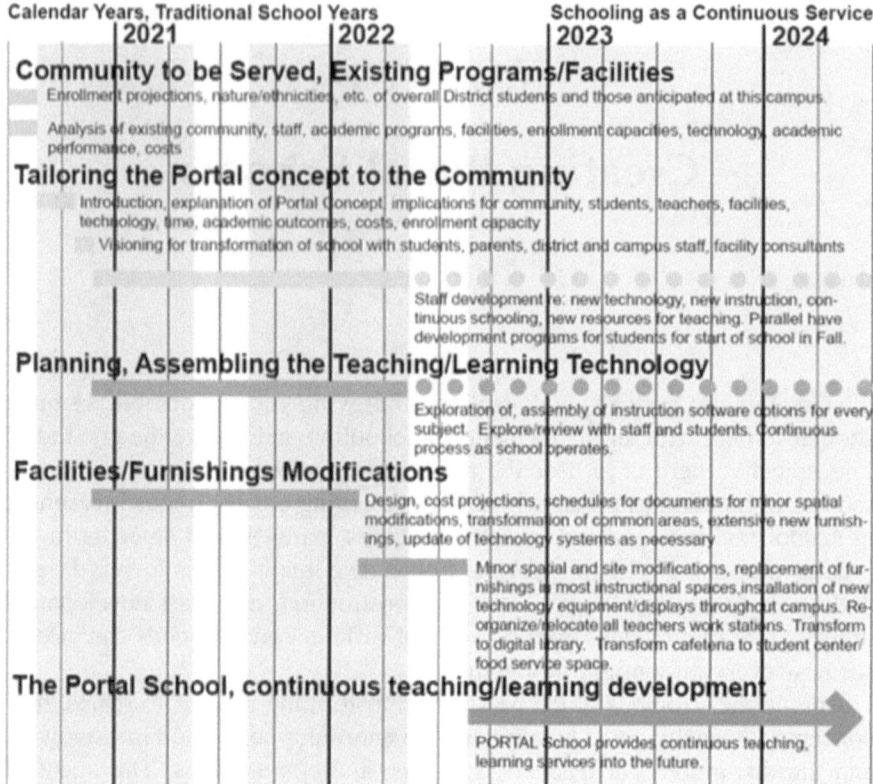

Figure 3.1. Process schedule diagram for creating portal schools. *Author created*.

How homogeneous or diverse are those students likely to be in terms of their ethnicities, languages, family economics, community contexts, etc.—and what are the implications for future teaching and learning in the school? What is special about the school's community context in terms of businesses, offices, retail, cultural, and/or industrial areas, and what resources do these afford the school that might benefit teaching and learning?

How is the existing school facility organized for core instruction? How is technology being used? How do students access "library" resources? What career programs are offered? What visual and performing arts programs are offered? What physical education and athletic programs are offered? How is the school performing in terms of outcomes for its students, i.e., the percentage of graduates? What are the school's graduates typically doing after graduation?

The objective is to be certain that each portal school will be an integral contributing part of the community it serves.

TAILORING THE PORTAL CONCEPT TO THE COMMUNITY

It is critical that the school share with the community, parents, students, and the broader school district of which it is a part a detailed analysis of the nature of the community/students to be served, and the existing facilities and programs to be transformed. This must also include a detailed introduction of the portal school concept and how it will serve the school's anticipated community, students, and teachers. A very serious substantial program of sharing this collected information must be pursued.

With the data in hand, the district and school should organize a visioning process for those who are truly informed and committed to the school, including representatives of the district and community, campus administrators and faculty, parents, and students. Erin Lynn Raab observed that "asking the right questions is the most important part of problem solving." The vision should define the aspirations of the transformed school and articulate how it will realize the objectives for the students and the community ("Getting the Right Problem in Education," Erin Lynn Raab, https://medium.com/reenvisioned/getting-the-right-problem-in-education-cb7ad7d9147e).

Raab also noted, "In a democracy, creating a shared vision requires asking beautiful questions and inviting people from different walks of life to participate in a reflective process." In other words, it takes engaging directly in the practice of deliberative democracy. It requires a process, not a one-and-done solution or program. And it needs to happen at every level—from the local to the national ("If We Want a More Just, Equitable Society We Have to Re-envision School," Erin Lynn Raab, https://erinraab.medium.com/what-might-it-look-like-to-powerfully-engage-a-school-community-around-beautiful-questions-24512ad743d9).

Growing out of these data and this vision, the district and school should begin an extensive and serious staff development program so that faculty, students, and parents will have a full school year or more to prepare themselves for the new portal approaches and schedules for teaching and learning. Given that there is an existing school and faculty with whom to work, there should be no surprises for faculty, parents, or students when the portal school opens and operates continuously all year. Any issues of concern should be addressed during the previous school year.

PLANNING AND ASSEMBLING THE TEACHING AND LEARNING TECHNOLOGY

Paralleling all the efforts above, there should be a special team of faculty members and district/campus technology experts that focuses, for at least a full school year before the portal school starts, on identifying and purchasing technology to really make the school special. The quantity of teaching and communicating software (see chapter 3) is exploding. After the portal school opens, this team should persist in an effort to keep pace with the resources to serve students and teachers—and it should communicate with similar teams at other campuses across the district. No campus should be "behind" the others in its technology.

FACILITIES AND FURNISHINGS MODIFICATIONS

Given the minor spatial changes to be made to transform a traditional high school building into a portal school, it should be possible to do the actual on-site work during the summer months between two traditional school years. After the community analysis and visioning work are completed, the school, the district facilities staff, and an architectural team should prepare documents for any on-site work to be accomplished over the summer months.

Ideally, these might include minor modifications in some corridors and common areas to make them more open and inviting, and to support the installation of digital displays to make the school's common spaces much more interesting and informative. Depending on the nature of the school's digital network, some additional network systems improvements may be required to support the extensive use of digital technology by both students and teachers. The largest part of the interior work would consist of removing all existing student and teacher desks and installing new workstations for both teachers and students.

In each existing classroom, there would be a teacher/advisor's desk with lockable storage and guest chairs. There would be a workstation for each student with access to both power and the internet, and lockable storage. Each room should need no more than twenty student workstations because each room will be used all day every day by both a teacher/advisor and students—a much more efficient way to use the school's spaces.

CREATING PORTAL SCHOOLS

As clearly described by the Elements of Schooling, transforming existing schools or creating new schools is far more than just a "facilities" process. Reflect on how you've transformed and/or created schools as well as teaching and learning in the past.

- When your district's latest school, or your own school facility, was built or modified, were the teachers and administrators, parents and students, and representatives of the community substantially engaged in the process of determining what to do?
- Did the early discussions about the scope and costs of the construction include detailed reflections on the students to be served, the nature of teaching and learning, the way school time would be organized, and the technology and teaching materials anticipated for the future?
- Did the discussions explore the optimum relationship between the school and its immediate context and the larger community?
- Consider Erin Lynn Raab's observation: "The kind of community students practice creating together in schools is the kind of nation we will become" ("Why School Shouldn't Be Designed for 'Learning,'" Erin Lynn Raab, https://medium.com/age-of-awareness/why-school-shouldnt-be-designed-for-learning-db0192a41f20).

Chapter 4

Learning from Other Building Types

In planning for teaching and learning, it might really help to ponder other building types that illustrate very different ways people, spaces, and learning can relate to each other—and the implications these examples might have for making different types of schools all with more attractive, effective environments for students and teachers. The issue here is not that these other buildings have been hidden away, but that we've visited them many times with our "educator eyes" disconnected and failed to grasp how the ideas they embody could enhance the environments in our schools. Some examples explored here:

- A Gothic cathedral—Rouen, France
- A modern market—Central Market, Houston
- A public market—Les Halles in Dijon, France
- Project-based learning in architectural schools—Rice University School of Architecture, Houston
- Hospitals, doctors—Medical Services

GOTHIC CATHEDRALS

Gothic cathedrals are renowned for their architecture, sculpture, stained glass, paintings, tombs, etc.—all of which depict important things about the Christian religion and its history. One can walk through a cathedral and literally "read" the artwork for everything from Adam and Eve to the life of Christ, to saints, popes, and kings. As we get to know them, cathedrals become giant fascinating "PowerPoint" presentations. Could we use current technology to make schools as informative and as engaging for students and teachers—only constantly being updated? This illustrative example

Figure 4.1. Rouen Cathedral in France. *Photo taken by author.*

is the great twelfth-century cathedral in Rouen in Normandy, France (see figure 4.1).

Do not think this is about religion; rather, it is about a way of informing, stimulating, and invigorating—and that may well have been an objective for those who created these remarkable places hundreds of years ago. When cathedrals were built, very few people could read or write, and even fewer had extensive personal libraries or "internet access." So the cathedrals, inside and out, were literally covered by sculptures, stained glass, murals, etc., that told the stories of Christianity.

If you get to visit a cathedral with someone really knowledgeable (like Malcolm Miller at Chartres), they can describe each piece of sculpture, tell the story of each stained-glass window, and ultimately illustrate how these extraordinary works of art are really "cartoon strips" that tell complex stories via sequences of multiple images. Malcolm Miller has been giving lectures and tours at Chartres Cathedral since 1958. He makes the entire cathedral come alive.

The facade of the cathedral is encrusted with sculptures of figures in church history. Figure 4.2 features figures around one of the entrances. The tympanums over the doors often tell the story of parts of Christ's life. The arches around the entrances often have sculptures of various saints.

While cathedrals are organized around their spectacular, enormous central nave space, they are in fact a complex assembly of diverse spaces all related to the history of the church and religious functions. Could we make schools comparably rich, but also constantly changing, and therefore just as fascinating and informative for students to move about in and study?

The chapels and choir, and the crypt below, often contain sculpture and tombs of church figures. All tell stories. Could schools have information relative to historical topics, figures, and events and make all of these interesting and informative for the students?

Figure 4.2. Entry doors at Rouen Cathedral. *Photo taken by author.*

Figure 4.3. Stained glass inside Rouen Cathedral. *Photo taken by author.*

The nave and chapels almost always have stained glass which tells stories about church history (see figure 4.3). They can be very detailed and colorful and function *exactly* the way we use digital displays today. Instead of blank corridor walls with lockers in our schools, why not put up digital displays with visual info that faculty and students can change constantly? If we could make schools comparably informative about the world in which students live and into which they will graduate, we could make school facilities and their spaces interesting and informative for both students and teachers.

The images could be drawn from the community around the school and from the entire world. The images could relate to historic events and current news. Schools could draw upon all sorts of sources—teachers, parents and students, universities, businesses, professions, media companies, manufacturers, agriculture, financial institutions, performing/visual arts groups, museums, transportation companies, energy and technology companies, construction, retail, food services—the list would be endless.

These should not be advertisements, but informative displays. How can students imagine things to which they might aspire if they have not been exposed to them? Could teachers assemble images related to a favorite subject of theirs? Could displays relate to an approaching national holiday or major local event?

In your mind, set aside the religious nature and age of cathedrals and instead see them as gigantic works of informative, fascinating art.

- We've made school corridors blank spaces that are easy to maintain and that don't distract students. Could we provide, throughout our schools, digital graphic displays that change constantly with information relevant to the world inside and outside the school, to things on which the teachers and students are working, to fields of study and work students might consider in their futures?
- Why are these sorts of displays OK for people, including students, on urban sidewalks, in museums, shopping malls, and airports, but not in schools where we want students to be engaged and stimulated to learn?

EMERSION AND ENGAGEMENT IN A MODERN MARKET

Central Market is located in the heart of Houston and has a very clear focus—food (see figure 4.4). When shoppers first enter the store, they are in a small room packed with fresh fruits and vegetables, and there is no view of a clear path through all this to get to other parts of the store. But then they are blown away by displays with dozens of types of tomatoes and apples and pears and parsnips and mushrooms—and they stop worrying about where they are going.

Figure 4.4. Exterior of Central Market. *Photo taken by author.*

But as they wander about, they get a peek into the fish and meat department, which has by far the largest range of choices in the entire Houston area—and the process continues as they are "enticed" along from one area to the next.

Never mind that despite being fascinated by all they can see, most shoppers initially find the spaces confusing—they aren't at all sure how they are going to find what they want, or even the way out. But by the end of their first visit, they grow to understand and to really like the spatial richness and decide it is in fact much easier to find things than in a conventional store with long straight aisles, shelving, and signs, because the store is an assembly of small and distinct spaces. They find they can easily identify each area, and within that small context, they can readily find specific items. In fact, compared to a conventional store, Central has very little signage—your eyes and nose do a really good job of telling you where you are—and your appetite and curiosity pull you along.

Shoppers move through the store by actually walking through, not between, each food area—vegetables and fruits to meats and fish to wine, to chocolate, to spices and dried/canned foods, to dairy, to a bakery, to cheese and delicatessen, and to areas with prepared takeout foods. Shoppers are fascinated by always being surrounded by foods and displays—and quickly they start to understand the areas and how to get from one to another. In the process, they find the store far more interesting than conventional supermarkets, and that it is, in fact, much easier to find individual items within the small context of their "shop" within the store.

Could we make a school where students and teachers are always within an area identified by changing displays and activities related to the discipline housed there—and which is much more engaging, interesting, and informative than traditional schools with corridors, blank walls, and classrooms? Often the store has special displays and/or demonstration tables, with staff showing off something tasty, passing out samples, etc. They try very hard to connect with people and excite them.

Spaces are really varied (not the case in most grocery stores)—both in plan and volume. Throughout the store, the structure and mechanical systems are exposed. In some spaces (meats, fruits/vegetables), the "ceiling" is relatively low and painted out. In other spaces (wines, bulk foods/coffee/bins, canned/packaged stuff, cold/frozen/dairy stuff), the roof pops up, and there are clerestory windows and natural light.

It is interesting to note, when there during daylight hours, the surprise of seeing the light—it really changes the space. Whoever heard of natural light anywhere in a conventional supermarket? Would students and teachers like natural light in their school spaces? This also happens in the Dijon/Eiffel

Market (see the section that follows) around the perimeter and in the roof/clerestories.

Think about the nature of museums—mazes of connected spaces—visitors walk from space to space to see art hanging on the walls. Museums may be similar to Central Market where visitors are surrounded by, and immersed in, what they came to see. Schools are exactly the opposite. The walls are often almost totally opaque (sometimes with lockers), and even doors are solid, with tiny sidelights or glass panels—if any. The intent is to keep students from being distracted by things in the corridors—never mind that the problem is more related to boring "stand and deliver" instruction than easily distracted students.

Returning to Central Market, shoppers learn that it has a cooking "school" on a mezzanine overlooking the food displays below. The store has evening classes taught by local chefs for which the store's customers (aka "foodies") pay to attend—and the cooking school includes displays of cookbooks. Could a secondary school have "evening" classes with special subjects that would attract both students and/or parents as well as community folks to the school outside of typical school hours? Why not?

Once how Central Market works is understood—how it makes food and shopping so interesting—it is natural to wonder if high schools could be much more like Central Market in being a total "turn-on" just to walk through. Could they also be a fascinating maze to explore? A series of linked spaces by which to navigate and understand an educational, spatially complex facility and program?

The next question for a school is how to pass out "samples" like in Central—bites of cheese, sips of fruit juices, spoons of jam, croissants or bagels, etc. Could schools pass out cards or pages with info on things extracted from courses—things that would interest students—and explain why they should take a class, what they would get out of it, why they would enjoy it? Could faculty or folks from the community "market" courses/subjects to students? I cannot recall a single time seeing anything about a high school course before I was required to take it. The title was usually something "tantalizing," like Algebra 2, and it was required, so the school didn't seem very concerned about whether the students were interested or not.

How about some visually interesting, informative, and frequently changing "sales pitches" to help students learn about what they are to study and how it may be of value to them in their future? What about if something related to math showed how the math skills students are to learn relate to doing business, engineering, cooking, athletics, medicine, or researching things in the real world? What about displays related to fields of study students may wish to pursue in postsecondary studies? What about information on various careers that might help them reflect on their own futures and the very important choices they must make as they complete high school and select a university or a career?

If we helped students see the value and use of what we require them to learn, would they be more interested in the courses and therefore more inclined to vigorously pursue them? For teachers, would the process of generating these materials help them imagine ways to make their subjects/teaching more engaging for themselves and their students?

Clearly, this sort of thinking would work differently for different areas of study and schools. In PE/athletic spaces, gyms, exercise/weight rooms, and natatoriums could be open visually. Visual arts should be open at least visually—but probably not theater or music rooms. However, these areas could have monitors that showcase the performances and artwork.

This would work for all core subjects, including parts of most science labs, as well as foreign languages (displaying information about other cultures as well). In CTE spaces, schools may need to be mindful of safety, noise, or smelly stuff. This could clearly help in culinary arts, medical, legal, architecture, finance/banking, agriculture, some shop programs (must control noise—but that can be done), and visual arts/graphics/video.

Central Market is about displaying and selling merchandise by making it attractive, i.e., hooking people by showing them stuff—by activating their taste buds—as in "foodies." How can this be translated into making a school that turns kids on? It seems like schools should be loaded with stuff students want to know about instinctively—but we make schools and learning so unattractive because we want to control kids and their contact with things. How can we expose kids to stuff so that they will ask to learn more about it? Think about Ted McCain's project-based learning idea (*Teaching for Tomorrow: Teaching Content and Problem-Solving Skills*, 2005) related to getting kids to ask him to teach them about stuff he wanted to teach them in the first place.

What could we learn from shopping centers? They are vastly different from Central Market in that they are a collection of enclosed/secured stores with display windows facing into the mall. As folks walk through the mall, they see these displays of interesting items—then they have to go into the store for further information and contact. There are issues here related to the security of merchandise, but the attractive part seems valid and applicable. That is better than most schools, even if not as good as Central Market.

But the giant difference between a mall and Central Market is that in the mall, shoppers, like students in conventional schools, walk in "public circulation spaces" between and outside the shops—whereas in Central, shoppers walk through the shops and are constantly exposed to/immersed in interesting stuff. How could we make that happen in schools? No one can walk through conventional classrooms, but they could walk through "departments" for history, science, or art, alive with displays created by teachers or the work created by students—just like in architecture/art schools.

How are department stores alike/different from Central? Is there anything to be learned from department stores? Does the difference between clothing, electronics, etc., and food (as in Central) matter? The great thing about shopping centers is the enormous variety of merchandise to be seen—and while the tenants/stores don't change constantly, their displays change frequently, even seasonally. They seem much more like Central than shopping malls.

A mall is a "street" lined with stores, each with their own entrance. A department store and Central are both individual enterprises—one place with lots of subparts. Shoppers wander through the store moving from one merchandise area (shoes, men's suits, cosmetics, women's unmentionables, etc.) to another. They can see, touch, inquire about, and experience the merchandise.

Maybe the difference is between our perceptions of students and shoppers. We think of students not as individuals, but as groups/classes. We want to be able to control, teach, treat, and work with students in groups/classes—not as individuals. In malls, shoppers are individuals or tiny family/friend groups, all with varied interests looking for different things. It seems like schools would change dramatically if we could think of students as "learning shoppers," to be attracted to what we want to teach them.

If everyone (teachers, students, and parents) could learn the curriculum requirements, then could the schools act like there are "no requirements" and try very hard to "sell" subjects, classes, teachers, and the overall school itself to the students and parents so they will want to take the classes?

- Could teachers prepare "marketing" displays and online materials—and could related work by students be displayed to interest other students in courses they might elect to take?
- Could there be presentations and displays in the eating/snack areas?
- Could schools distribute info to students online via emails?
- Could some of the displays help students become interested in the subjects they are to study? Quadratic equations? Nutrition? 1492? Veni, vidi, vici? Global warming?

A NINETEENTH-CENTURY PUBLIC MARKET

The Les Halles Market near the Place de la Liberation in the heart of Dijon, France, was built in the nineteenth century. It is a huge space housing shops selling every manner of food, including vegetables and fruits, dairy and cheeses, meats and fish, spices, breads and pastries, wines, etc., all under one huge roof with lots of natural light. The street around the market is ringed with restaurants and additional booths/shops, and above them are residences. Overall, it is an intensely rich urban context (see figure 4.5).

Could we make a school that would give students and teachers such an exciting overview, and at the same time such splendid exposure to so many things the school is about? This would entail making schools part of their context and making them more open inside so that all their areas are exposed, with each enriching the other.

Designed by Clément Weinberger and Gustave Eiffel, the market is yet another example of an extraordinary space that could really excite students. In one way, it is an "open plan" school, in that at first glance it is one giant open space. But then it is clearly a big assortment of stores that share a space, and each has its own character and focus. Could we make a school in a similar fashion, where each of the areas contained is a specialized space for very different subjects, methods of learning, etc.?

Could each have displays related to the subject? Could each have specialized spaces for exhibits? Could each have specialized equipment (labs, maker spaces, technology, etc.) for faculty and students? Could folks (including students and faculty) move about the "school" and walk around, between, and through these areas and see what they are doing, see if they are of interest? Could these education areas have displays, just like retail displays, to inform

Figure 4.5. Exterior of Les Halles Market in Dijon, France, with orange canopies over sidewalk shops. *Photo taken by author*.

and attract customers/students? Could the whole place have banners and lights that visually fill and differentiate the overall space? Could we locate diverse food and beverage services throughout the building, accessible to teachers and students throughout each day?

Could a school like this exist in an "urban" context? Or what about in a suburban context as part of a shopping mall where schooling would be a live part of the community and therefore way more interesting for students and faculty—and contribute back to the community with things and activities created by teachers and students? Could we make schools more interesting and secure by integrating them with their communities and eliminating chain-link fences and security stations at their entrances with scanners and X-ray machines exactly like those in airports?

The Dijon market is very near the heart of the city. While it functions on the inside every day, there are special markets on some days that fill the pedestrian areas around the hall (see figure 4.6).

Inside the hall, there are individual "stalls" or "shops" focused on specific types of foods—vegetables, meats, bakery, cheese, wines, etc., and there are typically informal places mixed with them. The "shops" are all very different; they are created by the merchants to attract their specific customers. The high multilevel ceiling with its clerestory windows and iron framing really enriches the space.

Schools should display and "sell" subjects and classes, just as these folks show off their vegetables. It would be great for teachers and the school to figure out why students should study something—why it should be of interest

Figure 4.6. Interior of Les Halles Market in Dijon, France. *Photo taken by author.*

or meaningful to them. Having some geezers in the legislature think it is important may not suffice for students.

The Market's central clerestory helps provide orientation in the large space. There are small "cafés" scattered around the space, and we could do the same for schools and students; there would not be a need for a cafeteria with rigid seating and schedules.

Could we make schools that "sell" education to students, parents, and the community? In the process, could we extract from our urban community contexts an atmosphere for teaching and learning that makes schooling more relevant and that makes more people aware of what our schools are doing?

PROJECT-BASED LEARNING IN AN ARCHITECTURAL SCHOOL

There are 149 architectural schools at universities in the United States and Canada—and all have been using project-based learning (PBL) concepts since their inception. Technology has changed the way architects work, but characteristic thinking processes remain. Professors define projects/problems to be created/solved by students. Every project has many possibilities and many "correct" answers. The creation and exploration of designs is a wonderful learning process—and in the end, students and teachers join in "juries" and everyone discusses the merits of each student's work.

These students maintain digital records/portfolios of their work to explain to others their creative process, what they've done, learned, etc. Could secondary school teachers and students experience project-based learning by visiting architectural schools, meeting with faculty and students, seeing student work, and observing student/faculty discussions in juries?

Characteristics of Architectural Education

The term "architect" covers a very broad range of jobs and responsibilities—it is a legal title related to an individual holding an architectural degree and license, but it can mean numerous, very different things in different firms doing different sorts of projects.

Teaching and/or practicing architecture is inherently interdisciplinary, mixing all the skills and information architects employ—history, programming to define problems, design/problem solving, urban/contextual issues, structures, MEP systems, life safety codes, civil engineering, construction materials/details/processes, construction costs, legal and business issues. It requires broad knowledge and diverse skills. It inevitably means something different for each "architect."

Diverse modes of instruction are used in architectural schools. There are some conventional studies in classrooms and online—architectural history, structures, mechanical/electrical/plumbing systems, business/legal processes/regulations. Architectural design is taught in design studios by having students create architectural designs for buildings to serve specific purposes.

All of the students work concurrently to create designs for the same project, but there are always multiple design possibilities and no "right" or "wrong" answers. Students and faculty work together to explore options and to assess the results relative to the given project requirements, and the overall quality of the design relative to other projects in the class and school, and the profession.

Time in architecture school is both clearly scheduled and super flexible. Classes/studios typically occur in set schedules to encourage and facilitate dialogue between students, between students and faculty, and in group discussion formats such as interim reviews or juries. But architecture students typically have twenty-four-hour access to their desk/workstations and do most, if not all, of their studies for all their university courses there—and time is very flexible.

Design studios accommodate varied skills and paces by allowing students to work "flex" hours in their studios. After graduation, architects continue to do this to succeed in professional practice. Time frames are set by clients' needs and construction schedules, and architects must adjust to meet these varying needs. Architecture is not an eight-to-five, forty-hour-a-week undertaking.

Students are given design problems to solve, from/for which to create a building design. The wonderful thing is that such problems have many answers—there is no defined "correct" answer known by the teacher or anyone. Teachers support, suggest, and guide students. Teachers are more experienced in problem solving and design, but they still don't know an "answer" when they give the problem. Students talk to each other and share experiences trying to solve programs and problems. While the working time during the process is very flexible, the overall time for the project is set—just as schedules are defined in architectural offices to serve the needs of clients.

Learning is highly individualized via critiques. Teachers and individual students engage in lengthy, frequent dialogues and dubbed critiques, exploring what the student is creating. There is no "stand and deliver" in studios. There may be lectures in some supporting classes such as structures, MEP systems, art history, etc., but not studios. Students have personal assigned workstations in design studios. These become students' "offices" on campus—many do most/all of their studies in all their courses there. Architectural schools are almost always distinguished on university campuses by having lights on late into the night, every night.

In the mornings, students typically have core courses (English, math, history, language, structures, MEP, business, etc.) in other parts of the university—design studios are in the afternoon, typically three full afternoons every week. While these formal studio periods provide a lot of time for students and faculty to converse, most students work far more hours, including evenings and weekends. There are no lectures—the teacher goes from desk to desk for critiques—or the teacher and students gather in their studio for group discussions.

Studios knit things together. In addressing design problems, students must call upon real-world info, history, structures, MEP, etc., and they immediately see how these are part of the architectural process. Studios are inherently multidisciplinary, and students instinctively go in different directions—each wants their own "scheme," and they try different things to be unique within their class. Everyone sees what everyone else is doing. "Cheating" is never an issue.

Architecture schools often bring in people from outside the school/university related to the project to act as "clients" to help students understand the nature of the problems and imagine possibilities. These people could include the owners of the building type being designed or architects who know the building type or contractors who have built comparable buildings. All this helps students learn about the critical interface with clients—how their input is essential to the creation of the design and how communications are essential to get the owner's approval and agreement to spend the funds for the construction of the project.

Students have traditionally explored design ideas and concepts via notes, written programs, abstract diagrams, conceptual architecture plans, cardboard models, and perspective sketches. While these persist for initial conceptual studies, today they are rapidly evolving into digital studies and 3-D images of both the exteriors and interiors of buildings. Students may explore and see much more than they could have in the past and can communicate their ideas to their professors and colleagues much more clearly and thoroughly. Today's digital technology is a substantial plus for teaching and learning.

What are the implications of technology for architecture schools? While the studies architects must do for history, structures, MEP systems, business/finance, urban planning, etc., can be done online, the design studios and the environment they create are the organizing elements of architectural education that knit everything together. The discussions between students and faculty are very much like those that occur in architectural offices. Today's wonderful digital tools have not altered the discussions between students and teachers.

Students must learn to manage their time—big deadlines are set by faculty within the school year, but within that context, students have a huge responsibility to figure out the time needed to make it work. During the semester, there are interim reviews with stipulated levels of design studies to be created. Students must plan and manage their own time. In secondary schools, time is typically organized by bell schedules, which keep all the subjects moving along concurrently—but in architecture schools, time reflects real-world deadlines which require flexibility in working hours.

This relates schoolwork to architectural practice after graduation. Time is set by the client's needs, and architects/students have flexibility in how they work to get to deadlines—it is a critical part of the real world. But this is not like forcing students to learn on schedule with fixed hours and dates. Architects have more input into the process in that they can work with clients to set dates to meet everyone's needs. Architects typically start with clients to define critical dates and to figure out who does what to get there—this should be the same for students in secondary schools doing PBL. Students should draw upon any resources and look for any related examples, such as sources with space standards like architectural publications/magazines, etc. Teachers can help here by directing students to examples that may be of interest.

Architecture students/faculty have interim reviews where students hang up their work and discuss it with each other and their teacher, other teachers, and folks from outside the school related to the building type. These interim reviews are very important to give each student a perspective about how they are faring relative to their fellow students—and the students really try to excel because they are usually very competitive with their classmates.

At the end of the stipulated time or the semester, architecture studios have juries. Each student presents their solutions/designs to fellow classmates, teachers, other teachers from the school, and folks from outside the school with expertise related to the project type. Students typically "hang up" their work where all can see it. Students must explain it; others may ask questions and make comments. This is a great part of architectural education.

Practitioners have "interim" working presentations/discussions with clients, so these dialogues are very important to both architectural education and the practice of architecture. Discussions among juries must be candid whether jurors agree with or disagree with the student's design concepts, but the jurors must be constructive in their critiques and aim their comments at helping the students.

Schools of architecture typically have 3-D model shops for the creation of models of buildings in wood, cardboard, plastics, etc. They also have a print shop with plotters for printing large images for reviews, juries, etc. Students will have individual computers and software. The school will define the equipment and software to be used to be certain that the entire school can connect and provide access to all the supporting equipment for all the students.

This technology evolves almost continuously—in both architectural schools and the profession.

In secondary schools, having some of these graphics skills and related graphics machines could really contribute to making the school environment much more interesting and visually lively for all students. And it would very much facilitate students' maintaining portfolios of their work that would be more informative than just transcripts with grades.

There are 149 schools of architecture at universities in the United States and Canada that would welcome high school visitors interested in their programs. The following website contains links to them: https://www.acsa-arch.org/forms/CompanyFormPublic/search. As an illustrative example, there follows a brief introduction and images of Rice University's School of Architecture (RSA) in Houston (see figures 4.7 and 4.8).

Part of the original university when it opened in 1912, the Rice School of Architecture is located near the center of the campus in Anderson Hall. Every student has a workstation in a design studio that they typically use for both their architectural work and for all their other studies at the university.

Never mind that architecture is not obviously related to English or math or biology—but the project-based methodology used in architectural schools for generations could be a powerful teaching tool for high schools.

- Is there an architectural school nearby you could easily visit? See the list referenced in the text above.

Figure 4.7. Anderson Hall at Rice University in Houston, Texas. *Photo taken by author.*

Figure 4.8. Interior of Rice architecture studio. *Image courtesy of Rice School of Architecture.*

- Would it be helpful if you could engage your students in their own learning and in the assessment of their own work?
- Would it be beneficial for individual students if they could present and display their work for others in the school to see?
- Could students maintain digital "portfolios" as a way to document their work and to show others, including universities, what they've done?

MEDICINE/PATIENTS VS. EDUCATION/STUDENTS

The purpose here is to explore similarities and differences between the way patients are served by doctors and hospitals, and the way students are served by teachers and schools. Teachers and doctors must recognize the similarities and differences between the individuals they serve and realize good outcomes for each one. Students and patients have real responsibilities for their own success and must contribute to the process.

How do teachers and doctors inform and encourage their students/patients to assume their own responsibilities? Teachers/students and doctors/patients may need different periods of time for their learning and treatments—but how do hospitals and schools accommodate these differences? Various areas of study and various medical procedures require quite diverse technology, spaces, medications, and staff—schools and medical facilities must be able to provide and access diverse resources. How does each achieve the flexibility to serve the very different, constantly changing needs of patients and students?

The measure of education and medicine must be *outcomes* for students and patients. Providing education or medical services on time and on budget is not sufficient. How do teachers and students, doctors and patients, measure success—collectively and individually?

Doctors and teachers provide very important and very different services to us every day. How are they similar or different in terms of how they relate to the patients and students with whom they work?

The medical/education analysis that follows is organized around the Elements of Schooling explored in detail in chapter 2. The analysis relates to traditional secondary schools, not to the proposed portal schools.

Doctors often have long-term relationships with patients and get to know them well as patients/individuals. Time is also a function of the nature of a doctor's service—general practitioners versus specialists. General practitioners treat patients and guide them to see other doctors as their expertise is required. A general practitioner may work with a patient for years but see them only a few times each year.

Teachers in traditional schools tend to work with students for fixed periods, with classes/meetings daily (semesters, school years), but may have little to no contact otherwise—before or after. Typically, most students start each school year with new teachers with whom they've not worked previously.

Doctors are contacted initially by patients based on individual needs, illness, or symptoms. Patients may select their doctor.

Teachers are typically assigned by schools to classes of students primarily on the basis of the curriculum requirements and the school calendar. Usually there are no choices for either teachers or students.

Doctors work with patients to define the time allotted for and sequence of treatment, healing, etc. Doctors draw upon past experience and knowledge of medical problems in conjunction with the condition of the patient to estimate the time for each patient's treatments, but it is not otherwise set or prescribed.

Teachers in secondary schools work within daily school schedules (bells/periods) and school semesters/years (typically approximately 180 days/9 months set by the state)—schooling is typically not provided outside this structure. Required learning must be realized within these time frames.

Doctors work with individual patients to realize their healing, hopefully within the time frame the doctor projected, but if the time needs to be shorter or longer, the doctor and patient adjust and persist.

Teachers work within fixed school schedules for individual class periods, days, semesters, and years. Students must meet the learning objectives within those time frames to obtain credit and progress to the next course. Absent that, in general, the remedy is that the student must repeat the entire semester/

school year in another class of students with the same instruction, materials, and time. If time for students could be as individualized as time for patients, the entire nature of teaching and learning—and its outcomes and costs—would be dramatically changed.

Doctors (most particularly general practitioners) maintain extensive records about patients and their health over extended periods of time, and have that as a basis for looking to the future when diagnosing, prescribing, treating, etc.

Teachers (particularly secondary school teachers who are focused on individual subjects) have access to transcripts, but how personal are these? Do they provide background on each student and their family and include details such as individual interests, strengths, needs, etc.? Do teachers review transcripts and make updates for all new students each year? How well do most teachers get to know their students before the semester/year is over and the students move on? Do they get to know them well enough, and soon enough, for that knowledge to impact how they teach?

Doctors review medical records, conduct exams, have tests done, etc., and then prescribe treatments for individual patients and discuss with individual patients what is anticipated, including who is to do what, what the schedule entails, what are recommended activities/diets, etc.—and the doctor and patient can work together to track the treatment progress over time.

Teachers are knowledgeable about the subject to be taught, about learning objectives for the course, about teaching processes and learning materials to be used, about the roles of teachers, students, and parents, and about the relationships between these studies and the general course of the school year, other subjects, etc. But teachers are typically focused on classes of approximately twenty-five students for fifty-minute periods and how to realize the most learning for the most students. Opportunities and time are seriously constrained for focusing on individual students' special needs and capabilities.

Doctors' services and success are measured one patient at a time—primarily by the patients themselves and their families and friends.

Teachers' services and successes are measured more by the overall results for the class and ultimately by the overall success of the school. Texas Education Agency statistics such as TAPR reports are indicative of how students, in general, fared in their learning, but do they directly/immediately impact how teaching and learning works for each of the teacher's students?

Doctors use very sophisticated, up-to-date technology for testing, diagnosing, treating, etc. However, while technology continues to improve the treatment of patients, it has not substantially altered the doctor-patient individual relationship, particularly communications.

Teachers may use technology to significantly alter their roles and how they relate to students. For centuries, teachers have been the primary source of knowledge for students, with lectures being the primary method of conveying content. Today, digital technology can do a much better job of conveying content in formats significantly more interesting and effective for students, and in ways far more flexible for the learning needs of individual students. This does not suggest limited teacher capabilities, but instead emphasizes the power of drawing on the best materials from multiple sources for every student. The huge benefit is that if teachers do not have to deliver lectures, they can devote much more of their time to working with individual students to help each succeed. But does that, or will that, happen?

Doctors may amass and share databases regarding patients, diseases, and treatments/medications—and in the process be more effective in treating individual patients.

Teachers and schools can use today's technology to not only change instruction, but to substantially improve how learning spaces (see below) and materials/resources can serve students. Paper libraries are fading very rapidly. Textbooks are going digital and may therefore be far more flexible and more easily updated. Tiny libraries with out-of-date books in individual schools are rapidly being replaced by networks that link every student and teacher in every school to the world—and to the Library of Congress, Bibliotech Nationale, etc.

Doctors' offices and hospital spaces are very diverse in that they have the opportunity to create their own spaces suited to serving their individual practices and patients.

Teachers and schools have focused on the efficient delivery of instruction within school facilities and operating budgets subject to state standards and close public/taxpayer scrutiny. The primary instructional spaces of our secondary schools (classrooms) have changed remarkably little over the twentieth century. But with the changes that have already occurred in technology, the pressures are mounting from school-choice programs and from rising school costs with dubious results for the spaces of schools to change to serve teachers and students.

Doctors' services and hospitals are generally funded by their patients and their insurance carriers, but there is a huge issue in the United States about unequal access to medical services because of funding, access to insurance, etc., that is yet to be fully resolved.

Public schools and their teachers/operations are generally funded by taxpayers via property and sales taxes, but this can create inequities from community to community, and from school district to school district, based on the funds available for the students and programs to be served. How do we address these disparities?

Clearly, there are huge differences between practicing medicine and treating patients and educating students, but

- Would it be advantageous for schools to find a way to establish some form of the long-term relationship between an adult educator and individual students similar to the one between patients and doctors? If so, how can that be done?
- Could each student, throughout his/her entire experience at the portal school, work with a single adult educator/counselor about the student's studies and aspirations for postsecondary studies or employment?

Reflect on the "building types" discussed in this chapter, none of which are typical in secondary school "education," but all of which seem to have characteristics by which educators and students might be stimulated to learn. Have you experienced other places and wondered if we could do something like "that" in your school? Have you shared the idea with others? Tried it?

Chapter 5

Slow Learners?

Great Ideas and Great Schools Ignored

The purpose here is to note with clarity, and to illustrate with a few well-known examples, that numerous inventive books and schools have been created over the last sixty or seventy years and that lots of people have read these books and visited these schools—yet some of the very school districts that built them have not learned from them and have continued for years to operate and to build traditional schools with poor outcomes for many students.

School districts seem to see traditional schools as the "basic schools," and the new and inventive schools as somehow "special"—and therefore not for everyone. Recall in chapter 1 the Texas Education Agency stats for the Houston Independent School District's high schools: that HISD has nineteen schools with A and B grades that serve 18,942 students, and nineteen with C, D, and F grades that serve 28,639 students. Most of the A and B schools are relatively small magnet or charter schools with special programs, while the C, D, and F schools are larger, more traditional comprehensive schools.

How can the very same district operate schools with such diverse outcomes? Have they rationalized these disparities by arguing that these schools serve students from different ethnic and/or economic backgrounds? That it is OK for some schools to graduate almost 100 percent of their students while some graduate less than 70 percent? Can't we and shouldn't we make schools that realize good outcomes for diverse students so that far more students can be successful?

Sadly, one can imagine many readers getting to the end of this chapter and grumbling about omitted schools that they believe are also forward thinking, inventive, and realizing wonderful outcomes for their students. But that only reinforces the question above about how educators continue to operate traditional schools when we know of better options. This is important!

The following are some schools/concepts on which to reflect. Despite having personally visited many of these twenty-eight schools over the years, the bulk of the descriptive material below was downloaded from the schools' websites to be as sure as possible that the information is correct and current.

THE SCHOOL OF ONE HIGH SCHOOL

Cleveland, Ohio
https://www.clevelandmetroschools.org/so1

The School of One offers students a differentiated, individualized digital online educational experience embedded with both the academic and social/emotional services needed to be college and career ready. The program is "specifically designed to meet the needs of gifted, talented, and undecided students whose circumstances dictate a more personalized and supportive academic environment."

The staff works collaboratively with each student to identify academic needs, areas of interest, and personal barriers—and strives to eliminate them. Teachers and students work together to create a new path to academic, personal and social, and emotional success.

The School of One is a single collective high school with students distributed across eight sites (existing high schools) around Cleveland to allow students to attend the site closest to where they live. Each site consists of a single classroom within an existing high school, with one teacher and a paraprofessional and support staff. School of One students may attend home events and participate in sports programs.

HIGH TECH HIGH

Public charter
https://www.hightechhigh.org

Opened in 2000 as a public charter school to serve approximately 450 students, High Tech High has grown into an integrated network of sixteen schools serving 5,350 students in grades K through 12 across four campuses.

The HTH organization includes a comprehensive adult learning environment with a teacher credentialing program and the HTH Graduate School of Education, offering professional development opportunities for national/international educators. HTH is guided by four related design principles that set goals and a foundation for their approach: equity, personalization, authentic work, and collaborative design.

Equity

Intentionally diverse/integrated, schools enroll students through a zip code–based lottery so that schools reflect the communities they serve. Teachers recognize the value of diverse students working together and use a variety of approaches to realize diverse learning. The school has a strong focus on college entrance and college completion for all students.

Personalization

HTH pursues a learner-centered, inclusive approach that supports/challenges each student to pursue their passions through projects and to reflect on their work. The school fosters relationships of trust, caring, and mutual respect among students and adults through design elements such as small school size, small classes, home visits, advisories, and student collaborative work.

Authentic Work

HTH school projects engage students in work that matters to them across multiple disciplines and connects their studies to the world through fieldwork, community service, internships, and consultation with outside experts. The school's spaces are collaborative workplaces with small-group learning and project areas, relevant technology, and common areas where artwork, prototypes, and various artifacts of the students' thinking are created and displayed.

Collaborative Design

HTH teachers work collaboratively to design curriculum and projects, lead professional development, and seek student voice and experience in these areas. With students as design partners, the staff are reflective practitioners—everyone is still learning.

THE CRISTO REY NETWORK

https://www.cristoreynetwork.org

The Cristo Rey Network integrates four years of college-preparatory academics with four years of professional work experience via the Corporate Work-Study Program. The network includes thirty-seven Catholic, college, and career preparatory schools that serve twelve thousand students across twenty-four states and which together have had eighteen thousand graduates. It realizes a powerful, innovative approach to inner-city education that equips students from families of limited economic means with knowledge, character, and skills to transform their lives.

Through the Corporate Work-Study Program (CWSP), students earn a majority of their education cost, which affords the schools a sustainable revenue model that does not rely solely on tuition, traditional fund-raising, or government funding. At full enrollment (four hundred to six hundred students), the financial model has 60 percent of funds earned through the CWSP, 30 percent raised via fund-raising, and 10 percent gathered from family contributions (on average, $1,000 per family). Locally owned and operated, the Cristo Rey schools' national office protects the integrity of the movement and furthers school excellence. A Christo Rey Network school:

- Is explicitly Catholic in mission and enjoys church approval.
- Serves only students with limited economic resources and is open to students of various faiths and cultures.
- Is family centered and plays an active role in the local community.
- Prepares all students to enter and graduate from college.
- Requires participation by all students in the Corporate Work-Study Program.
- Integrates the learning present in its work program, classroom, and extracurricular experiences for the fullest benefit of its students.
- Has effective administrative and board structures, and complies with applicable state and federal laws.
- Is financially sound.
- Supports all students in accessing and persisting through colleges that match their achievements, needs, and ambitions.

P-TECH SCHOOLS

Public-private partnership
http://www.ptech.org

P-TECH has now grown to more than one hundred schools across eight U.S. states (New York, Illinois, Connecticut, Maryland, Colorado, Rhode Island, Texas, and Louisiana), plus Australia, Morocco, and Taiwan, with further replication underway.

P-TECH students simultaneously take high school and college course work and engage in industry-guided workforce development, thereby helping to close the gap between young people's college and career ambitions and the skills required in high-growth industries.

A public education reform model focused on college attainment and career readiness, P-TECH schools span grades nine through fourteen and enable students to earn both a high school diploma and a no-cost, two-year postsecondary degree in a STEM field.

Students' workplace experiences include mentorships, worksite visits, and paid internships. Upon graduation, students have the skills required to either continue their education in a four-year postsecondary institution or begin entry-level careers in IT, health care, advanced manufacturing, and other competitive fields. While the P-TECH model spans six years, students are able to progress at their own pace, enabling some to work through the model in as little as four years. P-TECH serves students from primarily underserved backgrounds, with no testing or grade requirements.

P-TECH is a powerful demonstration of a public-private partnership designed to help all students achieve at the highest levels.

KIPP PUBLIC CHARTER SCHOOLS

https://www.kipp.org

KIPP is a nonprofit network of 256 college-preparatory, public charter schools educating early childhood, elementary, middle, and high school students (from Wikipedia). Ninety-five percent of KIPP students are African American or Latino/Hispanic; 88 percent qualify for the federally subsidized meal program. Students are admitted regardless of prior academic record, conduct, or socioeconomic background. Eleven percent of KIPP students receive special education services, and 17 percent are designated as English language learners (ELL).

KIPP students are admitted through a lottery system. After a student is selected via the lottery and decides to attend a KIPP school, a home visit is set up with a teacher or the principal of the school, who meets with the family and student(s) to discuss expectations of all KIPP students, teachers, and the parents. Students, parents, and teachers are then all required to sign a KIPP commitment of excellence, agreeing to fulfill specific responsibilities, promising that they will do everything in their power to help the student succeed and go to college. As of the 2017–2018 school year, KIPP's national college completion rate for its alumni is 35 percent, comparable to the national average for all students and approximately three times the national average for students from low-income families (about 11 percent). Another 5 percent earned an associate's degree.

KIPP has extended school days, requires attendance on Saturdays, offers extracurricular activities, and adds three extra weeks of school in July. Most KIPP schools run from 7:30 a.m. to 5:00 p.m. Monday through Friday, and 8:30 a.m. to 1:30 p.m. on select Saturdays (usually twice a month). Students spend that time in the classroom—up to 50 percent more time than in traditional public schools, depending on the region—and doing activities like sports, performing arts, and visual arts. Many of the activities KIPP offers might otherwise be inaccessible to students because of cost or scheduling issues. Because of this, the extended day offers students and families opportunities they might not get elsewhere.

The KIPP through College Program counselors work with all their students as they apply to college, secure financial aid, and make a college decision, and continue to work with them after high school to help them navigate the social, academic, and financial challenges they may encounter while in college. KIPP counselors also work with KIPP alumni to facilitate access to internships and career placement opportunities that will set them up for long-term success. KIPP college counselors stay in touch even after college graduation by providing resources and support to help them be successful in their early careers.

CAREER PATH HIGH

An early-college high school in Kaysville, Utah
https://www.careerpathhigh.org

Career Path High is a blended-learning high school that integrates innovative technology and best-in-class education strategies to provide each student with a personalized learning plan and a direct pathway to college and career. It is a tuition-free public charter school with no enrollment boundaries, serving ninth- through twelfth-grade students. The school gives its students a unique opportunity to access a twenty-first-century college model with competency-based education, premier facilities, lab environments, and Davis Technical College's schools of expertise.

VANCOUVER ITECH PREPARATORY

https://itech.vansd.org

Vancouver iTech Preparatory is a grades six through twelve, early-college, STEM-focused program created and operated by Vancouver Public Schools on the campus of Washington State University, Vancouver. Supported by partnerships with business/industry and higher education, iTech combines STEM—science, technology, engineering, and math—with liberal arts by integrating art and design principles into research and problem-based learning.

A lottery process with a designated number of slots for each zip code helps ensure that iTech's enrollment reflects the demographics of the Vancouver district. Ten percent of iTech's enrollment is reserved for students in Battle Ground Public Schools because the WSUV/iTech campus is located within that district. Established in 2012, the school currently serves around 400 students, with plans to grow to 670 over the next few years. ITech's four-year (on-time) graduation rate is 100 percent.

BRIGHTWORKS HIGH SCHOOL

San Francisco, California

https://www.sfbrightworks.org

Believing the world needs voracious, self-directed citizens who see tough problems as puzzles, the school created a rigorous model for high school education—one that puts the individual child in the center of the learning experience. This way the students become creative authors of their education, empowering them to achieve their visions of their own futures and goals.

School days are comprised of a combination of group subject study, independent project work time, community service, camping, outdoor experiences, field trip adventures, and internship or apprenticeship experiences. Each student is provided with the time and space to iterate what they do and how they do it. On any given day, students might be dissecting Homer's *Odyssey*, a chicken's heart, or the meaning of life. The school's small collaborator-to-student ratios (groups of ten to twelve mixed-age students) allow the focus to be on learning in all forms so that students are honored for who they are, how they learn, and who they strive to be.

How Brightworks High School inspires and supports students:

- Through a rigorous project-based, experience-driven curriculum and interest-driven, deep-inquiry learning.
- By allowing students to witness their goals come to fruition through a combination of encouragement, challenge, and hard work.
- By providing clear and flexible boundaries in order to scaffold the development of autonomy, allowing students to ultimately chart their own paths.
- Through collaborators who afford constraints, manage students' expectations, provide encouragement, and aid in logistics of off-campus time that contributes to meaningful research and work exploration.
- Through students and collaborators: discuss, question, and consider, aiming to keep their minds open to changing opinions and new ideas both in our small school community and the larger, complex world around them.

CLINTONDALE HIGH SCHOOL

Clinton Township, Michigan
https://www.flippedhighschool.com

Flipped school model of instruction: Students receive their teacher's lectures at home and do their homework in class. Students work side-by-side with the school's expert staff. One-on-one time with students is up four times over years past, test scores are up, and students are more engaged. The school is "flipped out" over its fabulous results and is extremely committed to ensuring that all of its students and their families get the very best the school has to offer. Teachers do not spend a lot of time on classroom lectures.

Class time is spent developing critical analysis and higher-order thinking skills. The school's faculty are not only experts in their field, but exceptional facilitators. Faculty assess the needs of each student through personal conversations and assessment tools, then the school is able to create a personalized learning experience.

TEXAS CONNECTIONS ACADEMY @ HOUSTON

https://www.connectionsacademy.com/texas-virtual-school/curriculum/high-school

At Texas Connections Academy @ Houston (TCAH), high school students connect to an award-winning curriculum that meets national and state standards through the school's online learning portal. That affords families an additional choice to homeschooling that gives their students a well-rounded and free public school education online.

The TCAH virtual high school curriculum is fine-tuned to launch each student into a successful future. While math, science, English, and social studies form the core of the curriculum, TCAH also offers a wide variety of virtual high school courses that provide a solid foundation for whatever path graduates choose: attending college or starting a career.

Students who enroll in virtual high school classes at Texas Connections Academy @ Houston (TCAH) get the flexibility and support they need to succeed in every area of their lives. The 9–12 education features a core curriculum, including math, science, English, and social studies. Electives in varied topics such as digital photography, marine science, game design, and world languages encourage students to explore and grow to become well-rounded individuals. Honors and Advanced Placement courses provide the challenge needed for college preparation. Students can also prepare for the future by joining college and career clubs.

Each student follows a personalized learning plan and has access to school counselors who help promote academic achievement and personal development. Student interaction is a critical part of the overall educational process. While most of the instruction supports anytime, anywhere learning, students also participate in a live online classroom environment through LiveLesson technology. This is also the technology students use to turn in homework assignments and securely track their own progress.

To make sure that the graduating class of seniors is well prepared for the transition out of online high school, Connections Academy provides access to a full-time certified school counselor, assistance in academic plans, and college/career planning.

SUMMIT SCHOOLS

Washington Puget Sound, California Bay Area
https://summitps.org

Summit Learning uses personalized teaching and learning to empower students to harness their inner drive for success. Developed in partnership with nationally acclaimed learning scientists and researchers, the school's instructional approach inspires children and prepares them for life after graduation. By concentrating on the personal needs and abilities of both individual students and whole communities, the school has been able to create an environment that fosters success.

Summit Schools strive to reach every student and ensure they leave high school with the skills, knowledge, and habits they need to succeed. And the school is dedicated to giving every student what they need to lead a fulfilled life, one with purposeful work, financial security, fulfilling personal relationships, engagement in the community, and the physical health to engage in daily life.

The Summit Learning approach has three main components. These interconnected components are necessary to ensure that students are ready to live their best life after graduation. Each school builds these components into their schedule:

- Mentoring: ensures that each student is known and supported by a caring adult through weekly 1:1 check-ins.
- Projects: equips students with life skills that they will apply to real-world scenarios in college and career.
- Self-direction: helps students develop the ability to set and follow through on short- and long-term goals.

WESTSIDE HIGH SCHOOL

Omaha, Nebraska
http://whs.westside66.org
https://en.wikipedia.org/wiki/Westside_High_School_(Omaha)

Westside High School in Omaha is based on J. Lloyd Trump's 1959 book *Images of the Future* for NASSP. Trump thought it was a huge waste of time for teachers to give the same lecture five or six times a day. He proposed that teachers give one large group lecture—then spend the rest of the day working with individual students or small groups. The school opened in 1951 and went to the current instruction concepts in 1967. He proposed four modes of teaching/learning: (1) large group, (2) small group for discussions with ten to twelve students, (3) hands-on, and (4) independent study where students could decide what they needed to do.

The school has no classroom instruction. Teachers "office" in instructional material centers (IMCs) located around the library, each focused on a single core discipline. The IMCs also include library worktables where students may work during their independent study time and have access to teachers. The school has "modular scheduling," which divides the day into twenty-minute increments that teachers may group in various ways. There are no lunch periods. For juniors and seniors, the campus is open—they can go out for lunch and for other purposes.

KERR HIGH SCHOOL

Alief, Texas
https://www.aliefisd.net/kerr

Based on J. Lloyd Trump's 1977 *School for Everyone*, the school does not separate students into individual classes with an assigned teacher. In lieu of traditional assignments, students receive personal activity kits (PAKS) that include all work for the learning unit. Seminars and large groups provide opportunities for teacher direction and group learning. Students may seek out a variety of peer and teacher input while working at their own pace. After a student submits his/her PAK, he or she takes a test on the material.

Students may complete courses and move on in less than a semester, but they must complete courses by the end of each semester. In lieu of classrooms, the school has large centers for each core subject, including centers for art, business, English-language arts, foreign languages, journalism, mathematics, science, and social studies. It does not have competitive athletic programs. Unlike a magnet school, such as Houston ISD's DeBakey High School for Health Professions, Kerr does not have an official area of concentration.

Students usually apply to Kerr in their eighth-grade year, but applications can be accepted in later grades. Students and their parents must attend an orientation, and then students submit applications. Admission to Kerr is determined based on grades, student behavior, and attendance records. Traditional high schools in Alief ISD are assigned by a lottery to either Alief Elsik High School, Alief Hastings High School, or Alief Taylor High School. Alief Kerr and Alief Taylor are located across the street from each other; Kerr shares transportation with Alief Taylor. Kerr is consistently ranked among the highest-performing high schools in Texas.

BIG PICTURE COMPANY SCHOOLS, THE MET IN PROVIDENCE

https://www.themethighschool.org

At the Met, every student has an individualized learning plan incorporating the school's rigorous learning goals. Parents and mentors are active members of the student's learning plan team, working with the advisor to develop the best curriculum for that child. The Met seeks motivated and curious learners who are eager to pursue their interests in a real-world setting.

Met Students take ownership of their learning and develop academic skills by exploring a variety of interests. The mission of the Met Center for

Innovation and Entrepreneurship is to prepare high school students to be successful in college and in life by engaging them in the rigorous study of entrepreneurship.

The goal of the program is to create the best entrepreneurship program in the country for high school students. The Met is a network of six small, public high schools located in Providence and Newport, Rhode Island. The Met's individualized learning approach has proven successful in unlocking students' passion for learning. The Met empowers its students to take charge of their learning, to become responsible citizens and lifelong learners. The hallmarks of a Met education include internships, individual learning plans, advisory, and a breakthrough college transition program.

SCHOOL OF ENVIRONMENTAL STUDIES (ZOO SCHOOL)

Apple Valley (Minneapolis)
https://sesmn.org

The School of Environmental Studies is an optional two-year high school in Apple Valley, Minnesota. Also known as the "Zoo School" because of its active partnership with the Minneapolis Zoo and its twelve-acre site on zoo property, the school embraces project-based learning with an environmental theme. The school is organized around "advisories" that provide individual student workstations, an office for teachers, and a science lab. There are no conventional classrooms.

CARL WUNSCHE SENIOR HIGH SCHOOL

Spring ISD in Spring, Texas
https://www.springisd.org/wunsche2

Carl Wunsche Senior High School opened in 2006. The new school replaced an older school that was built and dedicated in 1939 on land donated by the family of Carl Wunsche Sr. The school has many trade-related courses for students who are seeking more information and education in four areas of specialization, including health sciences, technology, legal studies, and business and finance. Because of the school's focus on vocation, it does not offer any athletic activities, but students may elect to participate through the schools to which they were zoned.

For the 2018–2019 school year, Wunsche received an A grade from the Texas Education Agency, with an overall score of 90 out of 100. The school received an A grade in two domains, Student Achievement (score of 91) and School Progress (score of 91), and a B grade in Closing the Gaps (score of 86). The school received all of the seven possible distinction designations.

The school was recognized in 2007 by CEFPI's MacConnell Award and in 2008 by TASA/TASB's Caudill Award. In the 2018–2019 school year, there were 1,473 students: 26.6 percent were African American, 5.7 percent were Asian, 56.1 percent were Hispanic, 0.8 percent were American Indian, 9.2 percent were white, and 1.6 percent were two or more races. A total of 64.5 percent of students were economically disadvantaged, 8.7 percent were English language learners, and 4.5 percent received special education services.

EAGLE ROCK SCHOOL

https://eaglerockschool.org

Located in Estes Park, Colorado, with an enrollment of seventy-two students, Eagle Rock School implements effective and engaging practices that foster each student's unique potential and help them use their minds well. Eagle Rock School serves adolescents who are not thriving in their current situations, for whom few positive options exist, and who are interested in taking control of their lives and learning. The school serves to educate its students and to provide grounding for its professional development center work of supporting engaging, progressive education practices throughout the United States.

Eagle Rock is a value-driven school. A fundamental philosophy, "Eight Plus Five Equals Ten," has animated Eagle Rock since its inception. The eight themes serve as guideposts for the overall school design. These themes are monitored by the school's leadership team to ensure that they are alive and well in the school. The five expectations serve as the organizing framework for the school's academic program. Students have to demonstrate proficiency in each of the five expectations prior to graduation. The ten commitments are the values the school's students are striving to internalize as they live the experience of Eagle Rock.

The Professional Development Center works with educators from around the country who wish to study how to reengage, retain, and graduate students. It provides consulting services at school sites around the United States and hosts educators at its beautiful mountainside campus in Estes Park who wish to study and learn from the school's practices.

The curriculum at Eagle Rock School encourages student ownership of learning, demands documented or demonstrated mastery of graduation competencies (requirements), and allows for the individualization of credit toward graduation. The school's graduation competencies are based on the school's values ($8 + 5 = 10$) and specifically within the five expectations. It is distinct from the curriculums at many other schools in several ways. The goal is that every Eagle Rock graduate will be a productive, engaged citizen, ready and willing to make a difference in the world.

Consistent with the findings of the National Research Council, the school designs a curriculum that is "conditionalized." That is, instead of decontextualized facts and formulas, it designs courses that put knowledge and skills to use under conditions where the application would be useful.

Furthermore, the NRC supports an alternative to traditional scope and sequence where "problems are solved not by observing the natural landscape through which the . . . curriculum passes, but by mastering time tested routines conveniently placed along the path." "An alternative to the rutted path [scope and sequence] curriculum is one of learning the landscape." The school exposes students to the features of various subjects that arise naturally in problem situations.

Students graduate from Eagle Rock on the basis of demonstrated competencies rather than the more traditional "seat time" and grades. Eagle Rock classes are both ungraded and nongraded. In other words, the school does not admit students as freshmen, sophomores, juniors, or seniors, nor are they expected to graduate in any particular time period. It is expected that all students will remain at Eagle Rock School a minimum of six trimesters in order for sufficient personal growth and character development to take place to be an Eagle Rock graduate.

A curriculum must be a coherent whole rather than a siloed set of academic subjects. Further, the purpose of high school must be more than exposure to a narrow set of subjects established in 1892. The purpose must include mind and character. Eagle Rock's expectations were established as five characteristics that would produce a graduate prepared to make a difference in the world. They emphasize academics, personal growth, and community values.

Students graduate when they are able to demonstrate mastery of the requirements, a process that does not require grades, only evidence of whether or not the students have achieved mastery. Although most students earn credit through course work, other activities such as teaching a class, participation in service projects off campus, or independent study plans serve occasionally as mechanisms for earning credit.

Competencies are not "handed down" to Eagle Rock to follow but were custom crafted to fit the mission and purpose of Eagle Rock School.

Graduation competencies (requirements) were created by instructional specialists (IS) and administrators knowledgeable in various disciplines with reference to the Colorado academic standards, as well as published lists of standards by professional groups such as the National Council of Teachers of Mathematics.

The Eagle Rock School's five expectations are:

- Communicating effectively: The primary purpose of the course is to help students understand how to get a message across (e.g., poetry, music, or art class).
- Expanding knowledge base: Help students understand and provide the tools to learn how to learn . . . able to apply to other situations (e.g., problem-solving course).
- Engaged global citizen: Help students learn something to better interact with various people and cultures (e.g., second language, worker's rights course).
- Leadership for justice: Help students understand what it takes to make a place (ERS, city, country) more fair and equitable (e.g., a restorative justice course).
- Creating healthy life choices: Help students understand that decisions they make can increase or decrease positive outcomes regarding the health of self, society, others, or the environment (e.g., you are what you eat, or a Riverwatch course).

KAHN ACADEMY

https://www.khanacademy.org

Salman Kahn founded Khan Academy as a 501(c)(3) nonprofit organization in 2008. Khan Academy offers free lessons in math, history, grammar, physics, biology, and many more subjects. Since 2015, Khan Academy has been the official SAT preparation website which high school students may use for free. Teachers use Khan Academy to make assignments, track student progress, identify gaps in learning, and provide tailored instruction. Today more than sixty-one million registered users access Khan Academy in dozens of languages in more than 190 countries.

The organization produces short lessons in the form of videos. Its website also includes supplementary practice exercises and materials for educators. All resources are available for free to users of the website and app. Khan Academy videos have been translated into several languages, with close to twenty thousand subtitle translations available. Khan Lab School, a school associated with Khan Academy, opened in September 2014 in Mountain View, California.

Teachers can set up a classroom within Khan Academy. This classroom allows teachers to assign courses within Khan Academy's database to their students. Teachers can also track their students' progress as they work through the assigned tutorials. Khan Academy positions itself as a supplement to in-class learning, with the ability to improve the effectiveness of teachers by freeing them from traditional lectures and giving them more time to tend to individual students' needs.

MANOR NEW TECHNOLOGY HIGH SCHOOL

Manor, Texas
https://www.manorisd.net

When the doors opened in August 2007 at Manor New Tech High School (MNTHS), 160 nervous students crossed the educational threshold into a school that focused on their potential futures in the fields of science, technology, engineering, and mathematics. Manor New Tech, built on the New Technology Network model of project-based learning, is strikingly different from what is found in traditional secondary education classroom settings.

The MNTHS student population is made up of applicants accepted through a blind lottery. As a result, the student population at MNTHS is diverse in all aspects, including the two largest subpopulations of young men and young women of color. Additionally, the project-based learning environment sets up an atmosphere where learning is student driven, engaging, and meets the needs of a wide variety of academic abilities.

Manor New Technology High School is modeled after Sacramento New Tech High School, which was modeled from the first New Technology High School, Napa. The goal of Manor New Technology High School is to prepare students to excel in an information-based and technologically advanced society. The school is committed to leading educational reform, and its instructional program encourages students to learn through collaboration with peers, businesses, and the community. Students develop problem-solving skills, interpersonal skills, and the resiliency they need to succeed in a rapidly changing and competitive world.

MNTHS's curriculum brings together the strength of modern technology, community partnerships, problem solving, interdisciplinary instruction, and global perspectives in a student-centered, collaborative, project-based community. New Tech schools use project-based learning and cutting-edge technology throughout the campus to engage students on a new level. New Tech Network Schools consistently outperform national comparison groups on measures of higher-order thinking skills, high school graduation rates, and college enrollment rates.

At New Tech Network schools, students are solvers and creators. They learn to communicate and collaborate. Through challenging, authentic projects, they learn to adapt and engage in the world around them.

FLORIDA VIRTUAL SCHOOL

Grades 9–12

https://www.flvs.net

Florida Virtual School (FLVS) was founded in 1997 as the first statewide internet-based public high school in the United States. In 2000, FLVS was established as an independent educational entity by the Florida legislature. Recognized as its own district within the state, it provides online instruction to Florida students in kindergarten through twelfth grade.

According to its website, "FLVS is part of the Florida public education system and serves students in all 67 Florida districts. FLVS also serves students, schools, and districts around the nation through tuition-based instruction, curriculum provision, and training." As a public school, its funding is tied directly to student performance.

Whether you live in Florida or beyond, you can access more than 190 courses with FLVS, from algebra to AP art history, and everything in between. The courses are real—just like the certified teachers who teach them. Public, private, and homeschool students from kindergarten through twelfth grade use the courses to succeed on their own time and schedules.

The Chugach School District
https://www.chugachschooldistrict.com

Chugach is a school district headquartered in Anchorage, Alaska. It operates three brick-and-mortar schools in Prince William Sound, Alaska, a homeschool program that serves students across the state, and a short-term residential school out of Anchorage. The three brick-and-mortar schools of Chenega Bay, Tatitlek, and Whittier encompass an area of 22,000 square miles (57,000 km^2) across South Central Alaska.

Performance-Based Education

Chugach is recognized as being one of the longest-running, public performance-based school districts. This model is described as a "reversal" of the traditional education equation. Instead of time being the constant and learning the variable, as in the traditional system, learning is the constant and time is the variable.

The Chugach School District recognizes and represents the innovative, creative, and diligent spirit for which Alaska is known. Driven by the community's desires for change and greater outcomes, the district continues to be a leader in performance-based education. Using not only its school buildings but its communities as its classrooms, the school's students demonstrate proficiency toward educational standards in many ways and progress toward graduation and successful careers at their own pace.

We have removed the organizational structures that are driven by time and age and replaced them with learning as the constant for which we strive. The school has proven the validity and value of this model over the course of the last twenty plus years.

DIPLOMA PLUS

diplomaplus.net

Diploma Plus was developed by Commonwealth Corporation in 1996 as a response to the alarmingly high dropout rate and barriers to postsecondary success for urban youth of color, and the inadequate supply of high-quality alternatives to traditional high schools. In 2003, Diploma Plus became part of the Association for High School Innovation, formerly the Alternative High School Initiative.

More than 83 percent of DP students are African American or Latino/Hispanic; more than 74 percent are eligible for the federally subsidized meal program. Students are accepted regardless of prior academic record, conduct, or socioeconomic background. When compared to schools with a similar student population, Diploma Plus schools tend to have higher attendance rates, retention rates, and passing rates on state tests.

Since its launch in 1996, Diploma Plus has grown from a one-hundred-student pilot at two sites in Boston, Massachusetts, to an organization that, in 2009–2010, enrolled over 3,400 students at twenty-nine alternative high schools across the country. Each Diploma Plus school is required to implement four essential components:

1. A performance-based system that includes competency-based assessment and performance-based promotion.
2. A supportive school culture that intentionally creates positive relationships among students, staff, and parents/families.
3. A future focus that provides postsecondary education preparation, career preparation, and civic engagement opportunities.
4. Effective internal and external capabilities to successfully implement the DP model.

NEW YORK PERFORMANCE STANDARDS CONSORTIUM

http://www.performanceassessment.org

The New York Performance Standards Consortium was founded two decades ago on the belief that there was a better way to assess student learning than dependence on standardized testing. Instead of basing a student's future on a one-day (or two- or three-day) test, an assessment system should reflect a fuller picture of what students know and can do. The consortium's system is based on in-depth literacy, mathematical problem solving, application of the scientific method, social studies research, a span of mediums for exhibiting learning, and a chance for students to have a voice and proud ownership of their work.

At present, nearly thirty thousand students attend the consortium's thirty-eight schools located in New York City, Rochester, and Ithaca, New York. A unique system: The foundation of the consortium assessment system—what makes it distinct from all other systems currently labeled as performance assessment—is the professionalism of its teachers and the opportunity for student voice and choice. None of these vital components is possible in an assessment system that is prepackaged, top-down, standardized, and unresponsive to the dynamic life of the classroom.

In the consortium system, the assessment tasks grow out of the curriculum. They are not imposed on curriculum, a process that must inevitably lead to the teach-to-the-test syndrome, whether the assessment is a task or a multiple-choice test. In the consortium system, tasks become possibilities for assessment only after students and teachers have studied the material, discussed and debated it, subjected it to their questions and writing, and thought about what might make an interesting choice for a topic or question.

The curriculum itself may undergo unexpected changes as a result of this process, with teachers introducing different books or journals or web materials to deepen the exploration of the topic, to respond to questions raised, or simply to help students understand an issue that has proven difficult for them. Out of this engagement and the relationship it develops in the classroom, both teacher and student become the creators of the task and take ownership of it. It is a meaningful and purposeful process, as opposed to the merely mechanical and formulaic response to "banked" or "canned" tasks.

The process begins with the student's entrance into the school, with its literacy-based culture—extensive reading and writing and discussion experiences in all classrooms—and builds toward the graduation tasks required of every consortium student: an analytic essay on literature, a social studies research paper, an extended or original science experiment, and problem solving at higher levels of mathematics. (Each school may also add tasks in the arts, art criticism, foreign language, internship, or other areas.)

In addition, a series of interim assessments, roundtables, oral argumentation based on content and evidence, analytic as well as creative and first-person writing, teacher- and student-initiated assignments, independent and assigned reading, and hands-on projects all prepare students for their graduation-level performance-based assessment tasks, known as PBATs. Graduation-level PBATs are evaluated by external assessors using consortium rubrics for both writing and oral presentations.

Consortium teachers commit to the many layers of work and collaboration required to make the system functional. They design challenging curriculum and tasks, respond to student interests and needs, develop and revise rubrics, and participate in consortium- and school-based professional development.

Collaboration is extensive, from observing each other's classrooms, to visiting each other's schools and serving as external evaluators, sharing curriculum, and evaluating each other's work at annual moderation studies. The professionals who have participated in the consortium schools have a unique role to play in the ongoing history of education in the United States.

The Assessment System

The consortium's assessment system comprises an integrated set of components, each one vital to the success of the others and all dependent upon the professionalism of the teacher-practitioners, the extensive collaboration and support they provide each other, and the active participation of students.

1. *Student work*. Students complete written tasks that require extensive reading, writing, and revising and are then presented orally for external evaluation. The tasks grow out of curriculum and classroom discussions and allow for student contribution and choice.
2. *Graduation requirements*. Students must complete graduation-level written tasks and oral presentations, known as PBATs (performance-based assessment tasks), including an analytic essay on literature, a social studies research paper, an extended or original science experiment, and problem solving at higher levels of mathematics. Students must also take and pass the NYS English Language Arts Regents Exam. Schools may add on additional tasks, for example, in the creative arts, foreign language, and supervised internships.
3. *System accountability*. Teachers design rubrics across the curriculum and revise them as needed. They also participate in annual moderation studies (for reliability), evaluating not only student work but also the assigned tasks. Curriculum meets state standards, ensuring validity; predictive validity is achieved through college attendance data.
4. *Professional development*. Underpinning the assessment system is the extensive teacher-led professional development offered both by the consortium's Center for Inquiry and at individual schools. Consortium teachers and staff collaborate on curriculum and rubrics, design courses that are content rich and support student questioning and voice, author books and articles, annotate reading lists, and serve as mentors for each other, visiting classrooms, participating in PBAT presentations, and leading workshops throughout the year.

5. *External evaluation.* Student presentations are assessed by external evaluators using consortium rubrics. In addition, consortium schools are evaluated by department of education superintendents, members of the Performance Assessment Review Board (PAR Board), and are the subjects of research reports overseen by prominent educators from colleges, universities, and other education institutions.

IDEA PUBLIC SCHOOLS

https://ideapublicschools.org

IDEA Academy (Individuals Dedicated to Excellence and Achievement) was started by Tom Torkelson and JoAnn Gama in 1988 in Donna, Texas, as an after-school program to help combat some of the major educational deficiencies they saw in their students, focusing on student achievement and college readiness. It became a charter school in 2000 to serve grades four through eight, then expanded to pre-K through twelfth. In 2005, they created a plan to launch twenty-two IDEA schools across the Rio Grande Valley by 2012.

With the opening of eighteen new campuses for the 2018–2019 school year, IDEA served more than forty-five thousand students at seventy-nine schools in the Rio Grande Valley, San Antonio, Austin, El Paso, and Southern Louisiana. By 2022, IDEA will educate more than one hundred thousand students across the country. The campus in Donna graduated its first class in 2007, sending 100 percent of graduates to college. In 2018–2019, IDEA graduated more than 1,185 seniors from fifteen campuses, and for the thirteenth consecutive year, 100 percent of seniors were accepted to college.

Starting in sixth grade, IDEA Public Schools' program, called BetterIDEA, is comprised of two components—the new core curriculum and the hybrid-learning component that provides individualized learning for all students. The new core curriculum is powered by Direct Instruction (DI), which emphasizes carefully planned lessons focused on learning in small increments. With clear instruction and teaching to mastery, teachers can accelerate learning for all students—high performers and students with learning disabilities.

Students are placed in flexible, homogeneous groups for reading, language, and math and are expected to score 90 percent or higher on daily/weekly assessments. Students advance only upon mastery of concepts—those who show exceptional progress can fast-cycle through if they show continued mastery of concepts. Students are individually assessed every five to ten lessons, and their progress is meticulously tracked.

The hybrid-learning component consists of two elements focused on a rigorous individualized learning experience. iLearning Hotspots on each campus allow students to work with math software that uses algorithms to create a unique learning path and pace tailored to each student. Accelerated Reader (AR) Zones are spaces on each campus that help students unlock opportunities and equip themselves for a lifetime of learning and enjoyment. With the AR program, teachers manage/monitor student's independent reading practice, and students are able to choose books at their reading level.

The vision for the IDEA secondary program is for every student to graduate ready to succeed in college—to enter their first year of college without the need for remedial courses in any content area. Students take AP courses to signal to college admission officers that they've taken rigorous classes and that they have what it takes to succeed in an undergraduate environment.

IDEA Public Schools provide personal technology devices to all students enrolled, including computers, tablets, and/or Wi-Fi devices, at no cost to families. For fourteen consecutive years, IDEA graduates have had 100 percent college acceptance to a broad range of colleges and universities across the country.

SARAH PYLE ACADEMY

https://www.christinak12.org/SarahPyleAcademy

Mission

Sarah Pyle Academy (SPA) is the "breakthrough" school program of Wilmington, Delaware. A unique program where students experience education through a blended-learning, flex model, with as much, or as little, personalized learning as makes sense for each student along their path toward graduation and "life after SPA." SPA meets all students at their zones of proximal development, creating a personalized plan to support their unique learning from that point.

Every student develops their capacity to demonstrate mastery of academic content and skills at their own pace, with the target for achievement set at a minimum of 1.5 years worth of growth, an accelerated rate. Students also participate in sixteen hours per week of aligned job/internship experience designed to develop students' career and college readiness skills.

Vision

Authentic and integrated technology practices are incorporated into every facet of the SPA program and are evident the moment students walk in the door. Students "tap" into school and internships using the web-centric, attendance-capturing Scholarchip ID badge, maximizing opportunities for flexible scheduling. It is common to observe SPA teachers using gamification sites to engage students in civics or seminar and watch students demonstrate science standards via a virtual laboratory. Integrated technology practices are used to personalize instruction, connect learning to real-life experience, and support goal attainment.

Digital Vision

SPA actively and routinely uses technology to access academic content, to effectively monitor and communicate student progress, to memorialize student award ceremonies for future viewing, to conduct/record professional development opportunities for staff and students, and to connect with teachers and staff during off-shift hours via Google Hangouts.

Students may participate in online content/curriculum platforms in goal attainment, with approximately 60 percent of credits currently earned using Edgenuity, 20 percent other web-based apps and interactive sites (e.g., Khan Academy and the Commons OER), and the remaining 20 percent project-based learning, traditional paper and pen, or other personalized method to demonstrate mastery of content.

Advisory Program

The SPA Advisory Program helps teach students more than just the academic skills they need to be successful; it helps them make connections between their academic course work and what they want to do with their life. Advisory also helps teach students valuable social-emotional learning skills, to help with personal wellness and teach students skills in areas such as conflict resolution, problem solving, and independent living skills.

K12 LAB, STANFORD D.SCHOOL

https://dschool.stanford.edu/programs/k12-lab-network

The K12 Lab aims to obliterate opportunity gaps in elementary and secondary education by designing new, more equitable models and sharing design approaches with students and educators. The lab serves as a catalyst for creative confidence in K–12 education through:

- Workshops, events, and resources for K–12 educators all over the world.
- Experiments with new educational models.
- Courses and other learning experiences for the Stanford community.

Workshops, Events, and Resources for K–12 Educators

The K12 Lab designs professional development experiences that inspire educators and set them on a journey to creatively engage with their students, content, school, and community. Through experiences, resources, and tools, we are constantly developing ways to build the creative confidence of educators.

We teach teachers in the ways they are now being asked to teach—in immersive real-world projects and experiences where creative problem solving matters most. Since doing beats talking about doing, we embrace jumping into new, invigorating experiences. Sure, there's some initial discomfort, but the reward becomes clear as educators stretch beyond their comfort zone to pick up new skills and mind-sets.

Experiments in K–12 Education

Designers on our team and in the K12 Lab network bring creative mind-sets and a bias to action to tackle big challenges, make new experiments happen, and share our learning with our communities to catalyze change. There are abundant opportunities for radical redesign in the K–12 sector. Some of the design challenges we've recently tackled include:

- How do we equip students to design equitable technologies?
- How do we make schools safe?
- How do we build awareness of the important role culture plays in learning?
- How do we prepare education stakeholders to navigate a changing future?
- How do we equitably scale education innovations?
- How do we move from standardized tests to measuring what matters?

Stanford Courses

The K12 Lab offers full-quarter courses and pop-out experiences for the Stanford community to explore the potential of design in the sectors of elementary and secondary education.

MIT MEDIA LAB

https://www.media.mit.edu

Founded in 1985, the MIT Media Lab is one of the world's leading research and academic organizations. Unconstrained by traditional disciplines, Media Lab designers, engineers, artists, and scientists strive to create technologies and experiences that enable people to understand and transform their lives, communities, and environments.

The MIT Media Lab promotes an interdisciplinary research culture that brings together diverse areas of interest and inquiry. Unique among other laboratories at MIT, the Media Lab comprises both a broad research agenda and a graduate degree program in Media Arts and Sciences.

Faculty, students, and researchers work together on hundreds of projects across disciplines as diverse as social robotics, physical and cognitive prostheses, new models and tools for learning, community bioengineering, and models for sustainable cities. Art, science, design, and technology build and play off one another in an environment designed for collaboration and inspiration.

A group of world-renowned faculty members and senior researchers lead the lab's research and academic program, working with graduate students, research staff, visiting scientists, postdoctoral researchers, lecturers, and staff members. In addition, numerous MIT undergraduates engage in research projects at the lab through MIT's Undergraduate Research Opportunities Program. The Lab and MAS program originated in a report to MIT's School of Architecture and Planning (SA+P) with which they share an emphasis on design, hands-on learning, collaborative research, and critique and reflection.

Media Lab alumni and researchers go on to careers in research and academia; to become entrepreneurs; to bring their unique skills and insights to industry; or to become independent designers, artists, inventors, and consultants.

Research and projects developed at the Media Lab frequently grow and evolve out of the lab, too: as spinoff companies, as exhibitions and performances, as tech transfer to member companies, and, perhaps most importantly, as the basis for continued research and exploration for others, both within the lab and all over the world.

HUDSON VALLEY SUDBURY SCHOOL

https://hvsudburyschool.com

Philosophy at Hudson Valley Sudbury School: education is . . . evolutionarily appropriate.

Hudson Valley Sudbury School's program is aligned with the deep evolutionary heritage of human beings. According to Boston College professor of evolutionary psychology Peter Gray, "For hundreds of thousands of years, up until the time when agriculture was invented (a mere 10,000 years ago), we were all hunter-gatherers. Our human instincts, including all of the instinctive means by which we learn, came about in the context of that way of life." Gray says that in hunter-gatherer tribes:

- Hunter-gatherer children must learn an enormous amount in order to become successful adults.
- The children learn all this without being formally taught.
- The children are afforded enormous amounts of time to play and explore.
- The children observe adults' activities and incorporate those activities into their play.

Gray's theory is that play came about via natural selection to serve the purposes of education. Our program aligns with these criteria, harnessing the deep instinctual learning habits of children.

Integrated with Real Life

Instead of carving out discreet periods of time to study basic skills like spelling and math, our students acquire skills within the context of their passions and responsibilities. Every one of them has interests, and—whatever they are—pursuing them at a high level requires the development of "hard" skills related to:

- Literacy
- Critical thinking
- Research

to name a few, as well as "soft" skills like:

- Patience
- Perseverance
- Confidence

Engaging with the democratic processes at school engenders interpersonal skills like:

- Listening and empathy
- Negotiation and compromise
- Articulation and communication

Often these skills are acquired as by-products, via processes resembling osmosis, while students single-mindedly pursue their interests, manage the school, and share resources.

Individualized

We all know everyone is different—so why does conventional education treat us as if we're all the same? We all have our own needs, proclivities, interests, and challenges—and our own genius or calling. The program at Hudson Valley Sudbury School meets each student precisely where they are, and stays right with them as they mature and grow.

Structure: we employ . . .

Democracy

Hudson Valley Sudbury School is a direct democracy; each student and member of the staff has an equal vote in managing all aspects of the school's operation. The structure and administration of the school is a reservoir of learning opportunity, and students learn firsthand the principles, processes, and politics of democratic governance. They balance individual and communal needs and experience autonomy and responsibility within a tightly knit and equitable community.

Self-Directed Education

The Alliance for Self-Directed Education defines the term this way: "Self-directed education is education that derives from the self-chosen activities and life experiences of the person becoming educated, whether or not those activities were chosen deliberately for the purpose of education."

Self-directed Education:

- Harnesses the power of intrinsic motivation by allowing students to focus on their interests (and acquire skills along the way).
- Cultivates strong reflective skills as students ask themselves, again and again, questions like, "What do I want to do now?" "What is my next task?" "Who am I?" "Who do I want to be?"
- Allows the school to act as a venue in which any curriculum and/or learning methods and modalities may be utilized, including off-campus learning (college courses, internships and apprenticeships, employment, etc.).

Campus

Hudson Valley Sudbury School is located on a parcel of sixty-seven wooded acres in the foothills of the Catskill Mountains in the Hudson Valley region of New York State. The campus is adjacent to the Bluestone Wild Forest and Onteora Lake recreation areas, which feature thousands of acres of public lands.

Consider the schools you've experienced, the books you've read, and other schools you've visited:

- On occasion, have you been amazed by the great ideas about which you've learned and how old they are—and then wondered why haven't others learned from these great ideas?
- Have you seen ideas that would clearly benefit teachers and students, but were somehow set aside because they required modifications to multiple aspects of your district or schools?
- Have you wondered if a great idea for teaching and learning could spread like the coronavirus—or have you figured out why beneficial, powerful ideas in education don't seem to be contagious?

Chapter 6

Epilogue

We should ponder here another reason to make schools more attractive—school choice. Public schools, magnet schools, charter schools, and private schools are giving students and their parents significant options in where they may go to school and in the nature of schooling they want, at different costs, at different schedules, and at different merits relative to postsecondary schools, etc.—and that choice is already impacting enrollments.

Houston ISD's enrollment has recently declined while the city's population has grown, and, to the extent that state and local funding are related to enrollments and bonded debt is related to bonds previously sold in anticipation of larger enrollments, this is worrisome. Until recently, growing populations reliably generated growing public school enrollments—but it is not certain this will be the case in the future.

How can public school districts take advantage of their size and diversity to offer parents and students schooling that others cannot match? Or are public school districts so self-restricted in their thinking that they cannot realize that advantage—that their competitors will seek out new and different approaches to schooling and further erode public schools? That seems like a bad thing for students, taxpayers, and our cities—and ultimately our future.

THE GLOBAL ENVIRONMENT AND EDUCATION

It was hard to avoid reflecting on all this while reading the April 2020 edition of *National Geographic*, which looked to the past and future regarding global climate change by including two "issues" in one: "How We Lost the Planet: A Pessimist's Guide to Life on Earth in 2070" and "How We Saved the World: An Optimist's Guide to Life on Earth in 2070."

The key issue in "how we lost the planet" is that we've known for decades about serious environmental problems, but not made changes we've known are critical to avoiding and/or resolving them. Recall the portal schools concepts and the list of inventive schools, books, and ideas and reflect on our schools today—and ask: "Will we 'save' our schools or persist with traditional education thinking?"

Index

advisory groups and small learning communities, 42–43
Advisory Program, SPA, 106
African American students: in DP schools, 100; in HISD schools, 11; in KIPP schools, 89
Alliance for Self-Directed Education, 110
American Dream, vii
architectural education, 74–75
architectural schools: displays in, 30, 43, 45, 70–71; PBL in, 27, 74–79; RSA, *78*, 78–79, *79*; SA+P, 107–8; time in, 40
art and music programs, 31–32
Asian students, in HISD schools, 11
assessment system, of New York Performance Standards Consortium, 101–3
attendance zones, 48–50
authentic work, 87

BetterIDEA, 104
Big Picture Company Schools, the Met in Providence, 94–95
Big Picture High Schools, 28
Bleske, Bernie, 49
Breaking Ranks (NASSP), 28

Brightworks High School, San Francisco, 90–91

Career Path High, Kaysville, Utah, 90
Carl Wunsche Senior High School, Spring, Texas, 95
cathedrals. *See* Gothic cathedrals
Central Market, Houston, *67*, 67–71
charter schools, 6–13, 28, 40, 49, 51, 85–87, 89–90
Chartres Cathedral, 64–65
Children at Risk, 20
Christo Rey school, Minneapolis, 47
Chugach School District, 100
classrooms, 41–42, 46, 92
Clintondale High School, Clinton Township, Michigan, 91
collaborative design, 87
Commonwealth Corporation, 100
communication, 26–27, 45, 76, 81
community, 53; portal schools and, 30, 43, 48–51, 57–59
competency-based learning, 37–38, 90, 101
Conference Technologies, 44
core studies and core curriculum, 32, 43, 92, 104
Corporate Work-Study Program (CWSP), of Cristo Rey Network, 87

COVID-19 pandemic, xi, 1, 18, 57; internet and technology during, 26–27, 35, 55
The Cristo Rey Network, 87–88
CWSP. *See* Corporate Work-Study Program

democracy, at Hudson Valley Sudbury School, 109
DI. *See* Direct Instruction
digital labs, 43
digital portfolios, 29–31, 43
digital resources, 24–27, 35–36, 46
Dijon/Eiffel Market, 68–69, 71–73, *73*
Diploma Plus (DP), 100
Direct Instruction (DI), 104
displays, of student work, 30, 43–45, 70–71
doctors, teachers and, 79–83
DP. *See* Diploma Plus
dropping out, 38, 100

Eagle Rock School, Estes Park, Colorado, 96–98
Eiffel, Gustave, 72
Elements of Schooling, 60, 80; as integrally related, 17–18; *Learning without Classrooms* on, 15; on traditional schools, 15, *16*. *See also* portal schools
emersion and engagement, in modern market, *67*, 67–71
enrollment: capacity, of school facilities, 42–43; at HISD, declining, 111; at HISD magnet schools, 21; by race/ethnicity, in HISD schools, *8*, *9*, 10–11; by student group, in HISD schools, *8*, *9*, 10
equity, 86
extracurricular programs, 39–40, 51

Florida Virtual School (FLVS), 99–100
food services, 47
"The Four Purposes of Schooling" (Raab), 21

funding portal schools, 53–55

Gama, JoAnn, 103
global environment and education, 111–12
Google, 26, 33, 36, 105
The Google Infused Classroom, 33
Gothic cathedrals: Chartres Cathedral, 64–65; Rouen Cathedral, 63–64, *64*, *65*, *66*; school environments and, 63–67
graduation competencies, 96–97
Gray, Peter, 108

Les Halles Market, 68–69, 71–73, *72*, *73*
Hechinger Report, 6
High Tech High (HTH), 86–87
HISD. *See* Houston Independent School District
Hispanic students: in DP schools, 100; in HISD schools, 10–11; in KIPP schools, 89
Homestead Act of 1862, vii
hospitals and medical facilities, 31, 79–83
Houston, Texas: Central Market, *67*, 67–71; demographics, since 1965, 6; population change in, 3, *4*
Houston Chronicle, 19–20
Houston Independent School District (HISD) schools, 3, 5–7; Children at Risk and, 20; digital libraries for, 34; enrollment decline, 111; magnet schools, 21; map of, 11, *12*; multiple campuses of, 22–23; problems of, *Houston Chronicle* editorials on, 19–20; student enrollment, by race/ethnicity, *8*, *9*, 10–11; TEA TAPR on, *8*, 8–11, *9*, *12*, 20–21, 85; technology in, 25
HTH. *See* High Tech High
Hudson Valley Sudbury School, 108–10
hunter-gatherers, 108

IDEA Public Schools, 103–4
Images of the Future (Trump), 28, 93
IMCs. *See* instructional material centers
immigrants, to US, vii, 19
Immigration and Nationality Act of 1965, 6
individualized teaching and learning, 75; at Big Picture Company Schools, the Met in Providence, 94–95; at Hudson Valley Sudbury School, 108; in IDEA Public Schools, 104; in portal schools, 23–25, 27–31, 33, 35, 37, 40, 49; school time, 81
industrialization, vii
instructional material centers (IMCs), 93
instruction methods, 32
internet, 26–27, 33–34

K12 Lab, Stanford d.school, 106–7
Kahn, Salman, 98
Kahn Academy, 98
Kelly, Frank, 15
Kerr High School, Alief, Texas, 28, 94
KIPP public charter schools, 28, 40, 51, 89–90
Klineberg, Stephen L., 6
Klinenberg, Eric, 6, 53

Lamar High School, Houston, 47
Latino students: in DP schools, 100; in KIPP schools, 89
Learning without Classrooms (Kelly and McCain), 15
lectures, 28, 34–35, 81–82, 93
libraries and librarians, 34, 41–42, 82, 93
Louisiana Purchase of 1803, vii

magnet schools, 21, 49, 85, 94
Manifest Destiny, vii
Manor New Technology High School (MNTHS), 98–99
Maple Ridge High School, 29
markets: Central Market, Houston, *67*, 67–71; Dijon/Eiffel Market, 68–69, 71–73, *73*; Les Halles Market, 68–69, 71–73, *72*, *73*; modern, *67*, 67–71; nineteenth-century public, 71–74, *72*, *73*
mascots, 51
mass instruction, in traditional schools, 24
McCain, Ted, 15, 27, 29, 70
McQueen, Michael, 55
medical facilities, 31, 79–83
Miller, Malcolm, 64–65
MIT Media Lab, 107–8
MNTHS. *See* Manor New Technology High School
modern market, *67*, 67–71
modular scheduling, 93–94

NASSP, 28, 93
National Geographic, 111
National Research Council (NRC), 96
natural light, 46
New Tech Network Schools, 98–99
New York Performance Standards Consortium, 101–3
nineteenth-century public market, 71–74, *72*, *73*
NRC. *See* National Research Council

Omaha Westside High School, 28
online learning, 29, 35–36, 39, 92

PAKS. *See* personal activity kits
Palaces for the People (Klinenberg), 6, 53
parents, students and: searching for schools, 52–53; teachers and, 23–25, 28, 38–39, 81; white, 3
patients, students and, 79–83
PBATs. *See* performance-based assessment tasks
PBL. *See* project-based learning
performance-based assessment tasks (PBATs), 102–3
performance-based education, 100–101
performance-based promotion, 101

personal activity kits (PAKS), 94
personal digital devices, 33–34
personalization, 87
portal schools, xi, *17*, 111–12; advisory groups/small learning communities in, 42–43; attendance zones in, 48–50; classrooms in, 41–42, 46; community served by, 30, 43, 48–51, 57–59; core studies, 32; corridors in, 43–46; courses/teaching in, 30; district structure, *50*; facilities and staff costs, 53–54; facilities of, 41–43, 57–58, 60–61; faculty roles in, 24; food services and dining spaces in, 47; funding, 53–55; instruction in, 23–32; libraries and librarians in, 34, 41–42; natural light, 46; PBL in, 27, 29; school costs, 54; "schoolday" in, 40; searching for, 52–53; spaces of, 27, 41–48; technology costs, 54–55; technology in, 24–28, 33–37, 42, 57, 60; time costs, 54; time in, 37–41; video monitor displays in, 43–45
portal schools, creating: concept of, tailoring to community, 59; existing programs and facilities, 57–58; facilities and furnishings modifications, 60–61; process schedule diagram for, 57, *58*; teaching and learning technology, planning and assembling, 60
portal schools, students in: art and music programs for, 31–32; attendance zones for, 48–49; attracting, 50–51; competency-based learning, 37–38; digital portfolios of, 29–31; extracurricular programs, 39–40; failure and, 30–31; grades of, 29; graduation goals for, 38; individualized schooling, 23–25, 27–31, 33, 35, 37, 40, 49; online learning, 29, 35–36, 39, 92; polling, 29; responsibility of, 27–28; school time and, 37–41; self-paced instruction for, 31, 41, 47
portal schools, students and teachers in: digital portfolios of, 30; digital resources for, 24–27, 35–36; parents and, 23–25, 28, 38–39; relationships, 39; responsibility for realizing learning, 28; schooling as continuous service for, 38–39; school safety and, 46–47; school time and, 41; spaces for, 41–48; technology for, 24, 33–36, 42; workstations for, 27, 34, 40–43, 45–47, 60
Problems-First Learning (McCain), 27
project-based learning (PBL), 70, 105–6; in architectural schools, 27, 74–79; in portal schools, 27, 29
Prophetic City (Klineberg), 6
ProUnitas program, 24
P-TECH schools, 88–89
public charter schools: HTH, 86–87; KIPP, 28, 40, 51, 89–90; in Texas, facts, 6–13
public-private partnership, P-TECH schools as, 88–89
public schools: charter, 6–13, 28, 40, 51, 86–87, 89–90; enrollments, declining, 111; student demographics, 2, 2–3, *5*, 5–6; taxes funding, 82
purposes for schooling, Raab on, 21

Raab, Erin Lynn, 21, 23, 59, 61
race/ethnicity, in HISD schools, *8*, *9*, 10–11
racism, 19
Ravitch, Diane, 20
Reed, Garrett, 20
Region IV Education Service Center, Texas, 5, *5*
Rice School of Architecture (RSA), *78*, 78–79, *79*
Rouen Cathedral, 63–64, *64*, *65*, *66*
RSA. See Rice School of Architecture

SA+P. *See* School of Architecture and Planning
Sarah Pyle Academy (SPA), 105–6
School of Architecture and Planning (SA+P), MIT, 107–8
school boards, 18–19
school choice, 25, 49–50, 82, 111
School of Environmental Studies, Minneapolis (Zoo School), 43, 95
school environments: building types for, 63–83; elements shaping, 15–16; Gothic cathedrals and, 63–67; hospitals, medical facilities and, 31, 79–83; modern markets and, 67–71; nineteenth-century public markets and, 71–74
School for Everyone (Trump), 34, 40, 94
school locations and school searches, 52–53
The School of One High School, Cleveland, 86schools. *See* architectural schools; Houston Independent School District schools; portal schools; traditional schools; *specific schools*; *specific topics*
school safety, 46–47, 53
school selection, 18
school time: in architecture schools, 75–77; individualized, 81; in portal schools, 37–41, 54; in traditional schools, 80
"School and the Tomato" (Bleske), 49
segregation, 19
self-directed education, 110
self-paced instruction, 31, 41, 47
shoppers, students and, 70–71
Slaying Goliath (Ravitch), 20
social-emotional development, viii
SPA. *See* Sarah Pyle Academy
spaces: for food services and dining, 47; of hospitals, 82; in modern markets, 68–70; of portal schools, 27, 41–48. *See also* school environments
sports programs, 51, 86
STEM, 88, 90

student demographics, in public school, 2, 2–3, 5, 5–6
student learning, assessing and measuring, 20, 101
students: African American, 11, 89, 100; in architecture schools, 74–77; Asian, 11; dropping out, 38, 100; high school as "stepping stone" for, 30; Hispanic, 10–11, 89, 100; Latino, 89, 100; parents, teachers and, 23–25, 28, 38–39, 81; patients and, 79–83; public school, demographics, 2, 2–3, 5, 5–6; school selection by, 18; shoppers and, 70–71; white, 3, 11. *See also* portal schools, students and teachers in; portal schools, students in
Summit Schools, Washington Puget Sound, 92–93

TAPR. *See* Texas Academic Performance Reports
TCAH. *See* Texas Connections Academy @ Houston
TEA. *See* Texas Education Agency
teachers: in architecture schools, 74–75; classrooms within Kahn Academy, 98; doctors and, 79–83; lectures by, 28, 34–35, 81–82, 93; professional development, at K12 Lab, 106; students, parents and, 23–25, 28, 38–39, 81; in traditional schools, 80. *See also* portal schools, students and teachers in
technology, 18, 20; in architecture schools, 74, 76–78; during COVID-19 pandemic, 26–27, 35, 55; in HISD, 25; in IDEA Public Schools, 104; lectures and, 81–82; in portal schools, 24–28, 33–37, 42, 54–55, 57; in portal schools, costs of, 54–55; in portal schools, planning and assembling, 60; at SPA, 105–6
Texas: public charter school facts, 6–13; Region IV Education Service Center,

5, *5*; regions and school districts of, 3, *5*; school search resources, 52. *See also* Houston, Texas
Texas Academic Performance Reports (TAPR), *8*, 8–11, *9*, *12*, 20–21, 81, 85, 95
Texas Connections Academy @ Houston (TCAH), 92
Texas Education Agency (TEA), 3, 6; on challenges for schools and school boards, 18–19; TAPR, *8*, 8–11, *9*, *12*, 20–21, 81, 85, 95
Torkelson, Tom, 103
traditional schools: as "basic schools," 85; classrooms and facilities, 42; Elements of Schooling on, 15, *16*; mass instruction in, 24; teachers in, 80; time in, 80; transformation to portal schools, 49
Trump, J. Lloyd, 35; *Images of the Future* by, 28, 93; *School for Everyone* by, 34, 40, 94

urban planning, 52–53

Vancouver iTech Preparatory, 90
video monitor displays, 43–45

Weinberger, Clément, 72
Westside High School, Omaha, 43, 47, 93–94
Westward Expansion movement, vii
white students: in HISD schools, 11; white parents and, 3
"Why We Should Rethink the 3 R's of Education" (McQueen), 55
workstations, for students and teachers, in portal schools, 27, 34, 40–43, 45–47, 60

Zoom, 27, 35
Zoo School. *See* School of Environmental Studies, Minneapolis

About the Author

Frank S. Kelly, FAIA, is an architect and planner focused for the last twenty-five years solely on K–12 education. He is a graduate of Rice University, taught in the School of Architecture at the University of Tennessee, and has served for more than thirty years on the Rice School of Architecture's Dean's Advisory Council. He has served on design juries for the schools of architecture at Rice, the University of Houston, Texas A&M, the University of Texas, and UT Arlington.

He has given more than seventy lectures at education conferences in the United States and abroad, including ASCD, TASCD, CEFPI/A4LE, NSBA, NECC/ISTE, USAA, TASA/TASB, and EduBuild (Australia). He was named Planner of the Year by the CEFPI Southern Region in 2009. He was elected to the AIA's College of Fellows in 1984 for his design work.

Education projects in which he had substantial planning/design roles have been recognized by McConnell and Caudill Awards, and TASA/TASB Design Awards. For twenty years he was a senior planner with Stantec, an architectural and engineering firm with offices on six continents.

He has extensive experience working with scores of school districts to create district-wide plans to serve changing enrollments and instruction for the future. His strongest focus in these plans has been on helping educators challenge their own assumptions and explore how they want teaching and learning to work in the future decades for which new facilities will serve.

He coauthored *Learning without Classrooms: Visionary Designs for Secondary Schools* with Ted McCain for Solution Tree and *Teaching the Digital Generation: No More Cookie-Cutter High Schools* with Ian Jukes and Ted McCain for Corwin.

www.ingramcontent.com/pod-product-compliance
Lightning Source LLC
Chambersburg PA
CBHW020126240426
43673CB00038B/610